Self-Mastery Of Mind And Emotion

Channeled by bj King

From the Spiritual Hierarchy

1st WORLD
PUBLISHING

Self-Mastery Of Mind And Emotion

bj King

Copyright © 2025 by bj King

Published by 1st World Publishing
P.O. Box 2211, Fairfield, Iowa 52556
tel: 641-209-5000 • fax: 866-440-5234
web: www.1stworldpublishing.com

First Edition
ISBN Softcover: 978-1-4218-3593-8
LCCN: Library of Congress Cataloging-in-Publication Data

This material has been written and published for educational purposes to enhance one's well-being. In regard to health issues, the information is not intended as a substitute for appropriate care and advice from health professionals, nor does it equate to the assumption of medical or any other form of liability on the part of the publisher or author. The publisher and author shall have neither liability nor responsibility to any person or entity with respect to loss, damages, or injury claimed to be caused directly or indirectly by any information in this book.

I dedicate this book to dear friends who have supported me on my journey Peggy Big Eagle, Mary Bosse, Carol Cook, Mark Ellis, Lou Fleming, Wendy Winkler, Mary Fuxa, Debi Goebel, Carrie Haberern, Kara Jacobson, Joyce, McIntyre, Barbara Pomeroy, Lynn Rhode, Pat Lowry, Nancy Dancing Rain, Joious Melodi, Marie Commiskey, Dru Marie Robert, Julianne Rae, Shelagh Schopen, Ruth Vandercook, Glenn Walbridge, Rosa Alvarez,Macy Jozsef and Nathan Lopez who have supported me emotionally and physically during my journey.

Table of Contents

1.

The Nature and Mechanism of the Soul

Our bodies were created by our souls. There is a soul in every Human form, and that soul uses the lower aspects of Humans simply as a vehicle of expression. The objective of the evolutionary process is to enhance and deepen the control of the soul over this instrument we think of as our Human bodies. The sum total of these lower aspects, when developed and co-ordinated are referred to as the Personality. The Personality is composed of the mental and emotional states of being, the vital energy and the physical response apparatus, and these "mask" or hide the soul.

2.

Multi-Dimensionality and the Oversoul

All of creation is sacred and alive; each part is connected to each other part, and each is communicating in a cooperative effort to evolve. The smallest and the largest forms of life are involved at the cellular level and at the level of consciousness in this evolution. Our physical senses present our unique version of reality, in which our beingness is perceived in one particular dimension. Our perception of that beingness is built up through neurological patterning, and is the result of one kind of neurological focus. There are other alternate neurological routes as yet not chosen by many. Our environment, family, government and religion have established our current sequential perceptions. These perceptions have locked Humanity into certain perceptions of reality. These structures were meant to frame and organize experience, but we mistook the picture for the reality that it represents. These structures demand recognition of the Third dimension as the only possible reality. Our sequential prejudiced perception can be altered, however, and is more flexible than we might imagine. At all times, other unperceived impulses bombard us. These impulses are either too fast or too slow for our usual focus to perceive them. Our recognition of these "not familiar" energies can be learned and encouraged. Many people refer to this ability as extra sensory perception (ESP). We are all designed and capable of these other dimensional perceptions. At a certain point in Human evolution, we were designed to begin to experience what some people refer to as psychic phenomenon in order to bring our attention to these other dimensional realities. That time is now.

Governments and religion try to preserve the status quo, to preserve their own existences, not for political or religious reasons, but to preserve the official picture of the Self around which they are formed. Fortunately for us, the structured reality in which that kind of Self can exist is breaking down. The official picture no longer fits or explains private experience. At this time, we are not only being affected by exterior conditions, but also by interior "seeds" planted by our souls, to explode at this time and to cause us to question the idea of the Third dimensional reality as being the only one and to question Humans as being the only sentient beings in the Universe. The blueprint for Humanity's future is seeded in the tissues and the cells of the species itself.

When I first began to have these seeds explode within me, I was within the structure of organized religion. I had the focus of God, Jesus, Mary, Joseph and the unknown quality called the Holy Spirit. I had never seriously considered reincarnation because, of course, it is not taught in the Christian religion. I had never seriously considered the soul, actually, or the difference between the soul and the Spirit. I studied the *BIBLE*, and the more I studied the more questions I had, which were not logically addressed by the priests and Church authorities. I began to question the theology and dogma of Christianity and saw it as illogical. This did not make me comfortable or popular. When the seeds began to explode so that a new reality could be revealed within me, it wreaked havoc in my life, in my thinking and in my emotions. I could no longer believe what was being taught by the Church. What was I to do? Where could I go to find answers, to find the truth? I cried out to God in prayer and asked God to speak to me directly. Since the only mention of God speaking to Humans in the *BIBLE* was to the prophets, this was a drastic move on my part.

When the communication began, during meditation, I wrote down everything I perceived in my mind. My normal thoughts were still there, but there was another set of thoughts, as if they were in my right-brain and my normal thoughts were still happening in my left-brain. At first, of course, I thought I was schizophrenic; even though I had asked for the experience I never really expected it to happen.

During the weeks that followed, I meditated daily, sometimes several times a day. In the original communications, I felt I was communicating with God or maybe Jesus, since this was my only reality. As the communications continued, one day I was introduced to several spiritual beings. The consciousness with which I spoke suggested that these beings were other members of my Oversoul. This was a concept I had never heard of before. It was said that some people would consider these beings their "guides," Angels, muses or daemons.

It was explained that the Source, or Creator God, had sparked off parts of Itself into large soul consciousnesses, and that through time, these large consciousnesses sparked off parts of themselves into the next lower dimension. Therefore, down through the dimensions between the Third dimension of Earth and the Source, each of us has other Oversoul aspects operating simultaneously in other dimensions. It was also pointed out that we had the ability, through altered states of consciousness, to communicate with these other aspects of our Oversoul family. This totally blew holes in the Christian doctrine I had lived by.

It was then suggested in the writing, that I research the work of a woman named Jane Roberts who had written several books with an aspect of her Oversoul called Seth. Reading these books and especially the novels she wrote about Oversoul Seven, not only made me more comfortable with the idea of the Oversoul, but also made me laugh. I highly recommend the Oversoul Seven series to you.

Having only the awareness in Christianity that the psychic or occult is to be avoided, I had no understanding of what it was to be psychic or the meaning of the word metaphysics. I went to the *RANDOM HOUSE COLLEGE DICTIONARY*.

"Psychic: Of or pertaining to the Human soul or mind; mental (as opposed to physical) outside of natural scientific knowledge: spiritual — a person who is sensitive to spiritual influences or forces."

I had seen psychics and fortunetellers around Jackson Square on a visit to New Orleans. I was sure I did not want to become an obese woman, with gray hair, wearing long dangly earrings, sitting at a warped card table shuffling tarot cards. The very idea horrified me.

"Metaphysics: The branch of philosophy that speaks of first principles or the ultimate nature of existence, reality, and experience, especially as developed in self-contained conceptual systems or extending beyond the limits of the physical and psychological."

That sounded interesting and not so strange and not what I had perceived "psychic" to be. Could there actually be a branch of philosophy I'd never heard of dealing with this strange multi-dimensional experience I was having?

I then decided to look up the words Spirit, soul, medium and New Age.

"Spirit: The incorporeal part of a Human in general or of an individual or as an aspect of this such as the mind or the soul."

"Soul: The spiritual part of a Human, regarded in its moral aspect, or as capable of surviving death and subject to happiness or misery in a life to come. The principle of life, feeling thought, and action in Humans, regarded as a distinct entity separate from the body: The spiritual past of a Human as distinct from the physical part." (That sounded a lot like reincarnation to me.)

"<u>Medium</u>: A person serving, or conceived to be serving as an instrument through which another personality or super natural agency manifests itself." By that definition, I would have to define myself as becoming a medium. Yikes, I wasn't sure I wanted that title either.

<u>Mystic</u>: I later learned that mystics have the intention to be in contact with their souls and the Source at all times. This felt better, so I accepted it as my intention.

"<u>New Age</u>: The ending of the 2000 year Age of Pisces and the beginning of the 2000 year Age of Aquarius."

Then for some reason I felt compelled to look up Catholic.

"<u>Catholic</u>: Pertaining to the whole Christian body or church. Universal in extent, encompassing all; wide ranging." This didn't sound like the definition of the Holy Catholic Church, as I knew it, but maybe this was the inference in the Episcopal prayer book, even though I had not understood it as such nor had it been explained by the priest in that way or, for that matter, in any other way.

I was to continue my education by reading the works of Ruth Montgomery, who, as a respected newspaper reporter, began to have experiences of receiving information through writing from what she called "discarnate spirits."

Although her works did not include information specifically about the Oversoul, they did explain many other spiritual subjects I had wondered about. I highly recommend her books to you.

I will refer to the Oversoul as the various levels of ourselves that operate in other dimensions between God and us. When I see a person's Oversoul, energetically, it looks like a giant fireworks display, with explosions or expulsions of energy being projected down or lowered from one vibration or dimension to the next lower dimension. When I first began to see the silver cord coming out of a person and flowing above them, I was intrigued enough to follow the cord and when I reached the next dimension of that person, I saw a connection to other energies, entities. Following it further into the next dimension, the same thing happened. In each dimension, there would sometimes be one, but usually several, beings connected to the being whose silver cord I was following. At a certain level, not always the same dimension, I would find the original entity that projected down the current incarnation, or current soul aspect, experiencing life in the third dimension.

We are projected into the Earth plane from a higher level of consciousness by a much larger consciousness, but for what purpose? It seems that in each incarnation the consciousness has the ability to expand, depending on the experiences of each lifetime and the awareness gained. The Oversoul oversees the life, but does not control it. Once we are incarnate, we come under the Universal Law of Freewill. We can choose to behave as we wish and to believe as we wish. We do, however, come with a purpose. The purpose is spelled out in the contract we make with the other members of our Oversoul before we agree to each incarnation. Once we wake up to this awareness that there is a purpose to life, and ask for help to achieve that purpose from our soul, or Oversoul, God, help will be given. The Oversoul, Angels and God are not allowed to intervene in our lives unless we ask; this is the purpose of prayer and meditation.

We previously existed in the Third dimension. Earth and Humanity are moving from the Third dimension toward the Fifth dimension. At the time of this writing, we are in the Fourth dimension, which Christians would consider to be hell. The Fourth dimension is also often referred to as the astral plane. The Fifth dimension would be considered heaven. Around Earth, vibrationally, other dimensions exist. Beyond the Fourth dimension, the Spiritual Hierarchy has set up an energetic barrier called the "Ring-pass-not." The purpose of this energetic barrier is to keep the negative thought forms of Humanity from polluting the rest of the Universe. This ring of energy is periodically tightened causing time, as we know it, to speed up. As the Fourth dimension is pushed toward the Earth by this tightening of the ring-pass-not belt, Humans will experience the results of all our previous thought forms needing to be transmuted or forgiven. We can do this by calling for the assistance of Saint Germain and the Violet Flame of Transmutation. Earth and Humans are evolving into the Fifth dimension. We are currently in the midst of the Fourth dimension, which accounts for the amount of disease, anger, fear, addiction, hatred, violence, murder, rape, deception and craziness we see being acted out around us.

Souls whose bodies die and that are not energetically attuned to anything of a faster frequency than the Third or Fourth dimension can become stuck in the astral plane or Fourth dimension. Christians would see this plane as hell. The reason they see it as a lake of fire would relate to the energies of the first three chakras energies of survival, emotion and sexual energy, which would be seen as red, orange and yellow. If a person, during their life on Earth, is consumed only with thoughts of survival or sensory experiences, it is possible that their energies would be too slow to make it possible for them to enter the Fifth dimension or higher; these dimensions would be referred to by Christians as heaven. Jesus is quoted as having said, "In my Father's house are many <u>mansions</u>." I believe He actually meant there are many other <u>dimensions</u>.

People who are addicted to a behavior or substance are usually feeding the addiction of several entities. The only way a "stuck" soul can feed its addiction, once it is out of the body, is by joining with (possessing) the body of someone who is practicing their drug or behavior of choice.

In communicating with the other aspects of our Oversoul, we can bring more and more consciousness into our bodies. It is possible for a higher vibrational aspect of our Oversoul to over light our bodies to give a speech, create a piece of art, music or writing when invited. It is possible to establish such a strong connection with a higher level of one's Oversoul as to have constant contact. I recommend that we strive for this communion. The purpose would be to learn why we are here in this particular incarnation and to make sure we fulfill that destiny. This level of our Oversoul also has the ability to become our guide, mentor, inspiration and receptionist with other souls and what I call our "gatekeeper." A gatekeeper is one who protects us from being approached by Spirits who do not have our highest good in mind or who are not from our same Oversoul.

Often in this dimension, we will meet someone else who is projected from our same Oversoul. When we meet these individuals, there will usually be instantaneous energetic reactions, which might feel either positive or negative. Often we will incarnate with other members of our Oversoul to accomplish a large group project. Since we most often incarnate with the same souls time after time, whether to balance past karma or to work on new projects, it is normal to meet other people who seem familiar to us. We might think of these beings as soul mates, kindred Spirits, or other Oversoul aspects. Richard Bach's book *ONE* is useful in understanding more about the Oversoul and simultaneous existence.

REINCARNATION FROM A PERSONAL PERSPECTIVE

At this point in my spiritual progression, the Oversoul was mentioning past lives and simultaneous lives, which I found very confusing in light of my Christian perception of reality.

Through a series of synchronistic encounters, I met a man we shall call Joseph. I had a positive, unexplainably strong reaction to this man. I was puzzled by my reaction to him, since he was overweight, blond and fair-skinned, all things that would not appeal to me in choosing a mate. He treated me as if I didn't exist as a female, which I also found strange. At this point, Spirit suggested that I experience a past life regression in order to find out what caused me to believe that I had lived before and would live again. I called the psychologist that was suggested in my meditation and asked if he did past life regressions. "Yes, occasionally," was his reply. I asked about the price of the session and he indicated it would be seventy-five dollars.

"Do you take credit cards?" I asked.

"No, but if paying is a problem, I do sometimes barter. What do you do?" he asked.

"I paint and do calligraphy," I offered.

"Well, I can't use those services, but I have been interested in trying a new technique I have with an artist to prove we can improve a person's creative abilities through hypnosis. If you are willing to come for four sessions of hypnosis for creativity and write up the results, I'll trade that for doing a regression for you," he offered.

I could hardly believe his offer. It sounded as if I were the one gaining all the benefits. I agreed, made the appointment and thanked him profusely. When I arrived at the psychologist's office later in the week, I was very nervous and unsure of myself. Dr. Ben is a huge, but soft-spoken, gentle man, who gained my confidence immediately.

"Four, three, two, one, you have now entered a state of deep relaxation. Your body feels heavy. You will begin to see colors, images." The psychologist's voice was smooth, relaxed, reassuring. During the first session of regression I saw myself as a black slave who was raped and beaten to death. I came out of the regression exhausted and depressed. The psychologist assured me that subsequent sessions were unlikely to be as difficult, and that I might want to consider that the reason I had seen this particular life was to let me know the price one might pay for being in servitude to another.

Since I had no intention of ever marrying again or working in the corporate World, I felt I had eliminated the possibilities of being in servitude in this life. However, that week before my next session, Spirit began to suggest that it would serve the soul for me to marry Joseph. I was distraught by the idea, especially since he did not seem attracted to me at all. The next regression gave me insight.

"Four, three, two, one, you have entered a state of deep relaxation. Your body feels heavy. You will begin to see colors, images." I floated through a purple cloud, then a yellow mist, and settle into yet another female form, more petite and fragile than the one my soul normally inhabits in this lifetime. Tightness in my chest let me know I was anxious, afraid. My hand smoothed the horsehair cushion of the train seat, my first train trip from Baltimore, leaving a family of ten headed only by my mother, no father image. I felt cast out, rejected, sold to the highest bidder.

The brakes of the train screeched and the steam hissed as the train ground to a halt. Chills ran up and down my spine as I braced myself against the seat. I was apprehensive about meeting this man I had been sold to by my mother as a mail-order bride.

My feet felt as if they were made of lead as I made my way down the corridor with my one bag, which contained my total life's belongings. My eyes searched the platform, and I feared he was not there to pick me up and I feared that he was. My dreams of the past month, since I learned of my plight, had been filled with rape scenes of abuse at the hands of some faceless man whose hands violated my body.

As I saw this tall, broad-shouldered, round-faced, bearded stranger with happy, twinkling eyes approach the train exit, I stiffened. His voice, tentative, masculine and yet melodious asked, "Becky?" I could only muster a nod. My voice escaped me, and my mind was wandering frantically in search of words to express my relief.

He took my bag and my hand, and gently guided me to a wooden wagon hitched to a beautiful bay horse. His huge, reddened hands encircled my waist and hoisted me into the wagon as if I were as light as a feather, but as fragile as an egg. Gently he placed me with respect in a position of equal importance on the seat, then climbed up beside me and took the reins masterfully and with authority. I observed, even in my fright, that he did not slap the horse with the reins, but made a gentle clucking sound with his tongue against the roof of his mouth, and the animal moved forward with knowing, understanding his task. The giant of a man then turned his full attention to observing my face, my hands and my hair. While he said very little, he communicated warmth through his eyes that I had never before experienced. His eyes seemed to hold some hidden message that I felt I would soon understand.

After two hours of travel through beautiful green rolling hills, we rounded a bend in the road and I saw a small log cabin nestled in the trees and heard the sound of a nearby brook as I sat in the stillness of the wagon.

Again, he lifted me effortlessly to the ground and took my hand to lead me to the stream. He motioned for me to sit on a rock that protruded over the water. After removing his boots and entering the water, he gently unlaced my high-topped boots and put my stocking-clad feet into the water, as if to ask me to remove my stockings would be premature, too familiar. His massive hands gently massaged my tiny aching feet, which had been encased for three days without the release for air. I was filled with awe, confused by my expectation in comparison to this experience, with a part of me still not trusting. I felt as if I were still dreaming, in a fairyland in the woods, my faceless monster having been transformed into a tender, gentle giant.

The next four days included his washing and combing my hair, showing me his land, massaging my back, nights of lying in front of the fireplace but having been transported from my nightmare existence to this on a bearskin rug, vividly expressing his dreams, his plans for our future. After all else and an established feeling of trust, his lovemaking was as gentle as any love I had ever created in my girlish fantasies.

I came back into my body from the regression knowing that this man was a previous incarnation of Joseph and that I would be safe to marry him. What I didn't know, but would later learn after only nine months of marriage, was that Joseph, even though he had been involved with spiritual studies for fifteen years, would find it impossible to stay married to someone who was psychic. I railed at my soul after this experience, feeling deceived and used. The soul explained that in each life we have Freewill and that Joseph's Freewill had to be considered, even though the soul would have chosen for the relationship to be otherwise. Through the years, many relationships have been brought, suggested and lived through for various reasons, many of which were karmic.

At this time in history, since we are moving from the Piscean Age into the Aquarian Age, it is necessary to experience many different kinds of relationships. The traditional one, marriage, or one romantic relationship per life is rare. We are finishing many thousands of years of karma in this one lifetime. Karma will no longer be carried over from one lifetime to the next in the Aquarian Age. We are on the fast track of evolution, between Ages, between planes and between the old and new version of the Human species. Time has sped up by the tightening of the Ring-pass-not; therefore, life is complex and much more will need to be accomplished, of necessity, during these lives we are living now.

Many people have asked for more explanation of the Oversoul. Not many people have written about this concept other than Seth through Jane Roberts in her *Oversoul Seven* series, which I highly recommend to you. I've also found some mentions of the Oversoul in Ralph Waldo Emerson's work and the Alice Bailey Blue Books channeled from the Master Djwhal Khul.

I came to know of the concept of the Oversoul from my own soul communication. Early on in my direct communication with Spirit, because I came from a Christian religious background, my knowledge of the Universe, Spirit, the Spiritual Hierarchy, Evolution, Reincarnation, The Intergalactic Federation and the Oversoul were nonexistent. Spirit has been gentle in expanding my conscious awareness once the first door between my conscious mind and Spirit was flung open in 1982.

I was totally blown away by what I saw and experienced in the regressions I experienced with the psychologist. It was impossible from that time on for me not to believe in past lives. I was then given a method by my soul of how to safely regress other people.

I did regressions of others for several years. I would put the person in a relaxed state and then guide them into the life their soul suggested to me through telepathic contact with their soul. When they began to perceive either images or awareness, I would follow along with them as they viewed the life to make sure they didn't get caught up in the story and begin to make it up. At the end of the session we would energetically clear the karma of the life, heal their cellular memory of the life and deliberately bring forward any talents or love they had in that life into the present life.

Sometimes people came back for more than one session. The first time I regressed a person and they showed up in a life that was during the exact time that we had seen them in another life I became very suspicious and unsure of the method. I challenged my soul for an explanation. It was explained that we carry the cellular memory of the lives that have been lived by everyone in our Oversoul. Because of this, it is possible for many people to believe they have been some famous person, such as Abraham Lincoln, George Washington, Joan of Arc, or a certain Pharaoh, etc. Once an entity has acquired a large consciousness and they transcend, they are then free to split their consciousness and project many aspects of their consciousness back to Earth for expanded experience. Because of this, we may have many other members of our same Oversoul on the planet at one time. These parts are spiritually referred to as "aspects" of one Oversoul or kindred spirits some; people refer to them as soul mates. It is also why we cannot tell a person how many lives they have lived.

It is not unusual to meet someone else from your same Oversoul. When this happens, there is usually a sense of familiarity with that person. This does not necessarily mean the encounter will feel positive. It is usually very highly charged, energetically. If we meet another person from our Oversoul who is a member of the opposite sex and of the same approximate age, the energy is often so strong that we assume the encounter is for the purpose of a romantic relationship, and many people jump into bed before they have any real spiritual understanding of what the soul had in mind for the relationship. It is not uncommon for the Oversoul to bring together two or more members of one Oversoul when one or more of the members are going through a traumatic or challenging change in their lives. It is also not unusual if the Oversoul has in mind a large project it wishes to accomplish through the aspects, which would require multiple persons or talents to complete the project.

When I first saw the diagram I'm offering you with this explanation, it helped me, because I am a visual person, to see many levels of what is going on universally and how many things fit together or operate. At one point, the Source made the decision to project parts of itself to create the Elohim, who are referred to spiritually as the Builders of Form. These energies are so enormous that they were able to project many versions of themselves into the next dimension. Each of these aspects is so large in consciousness as to desire to project more aspects of themselves into the next lower dimension. This process is repeated down through each of the dimensions between Source and the third dimension of Earth. It is also useful to realize that Earth is not the only planet where life is projected.

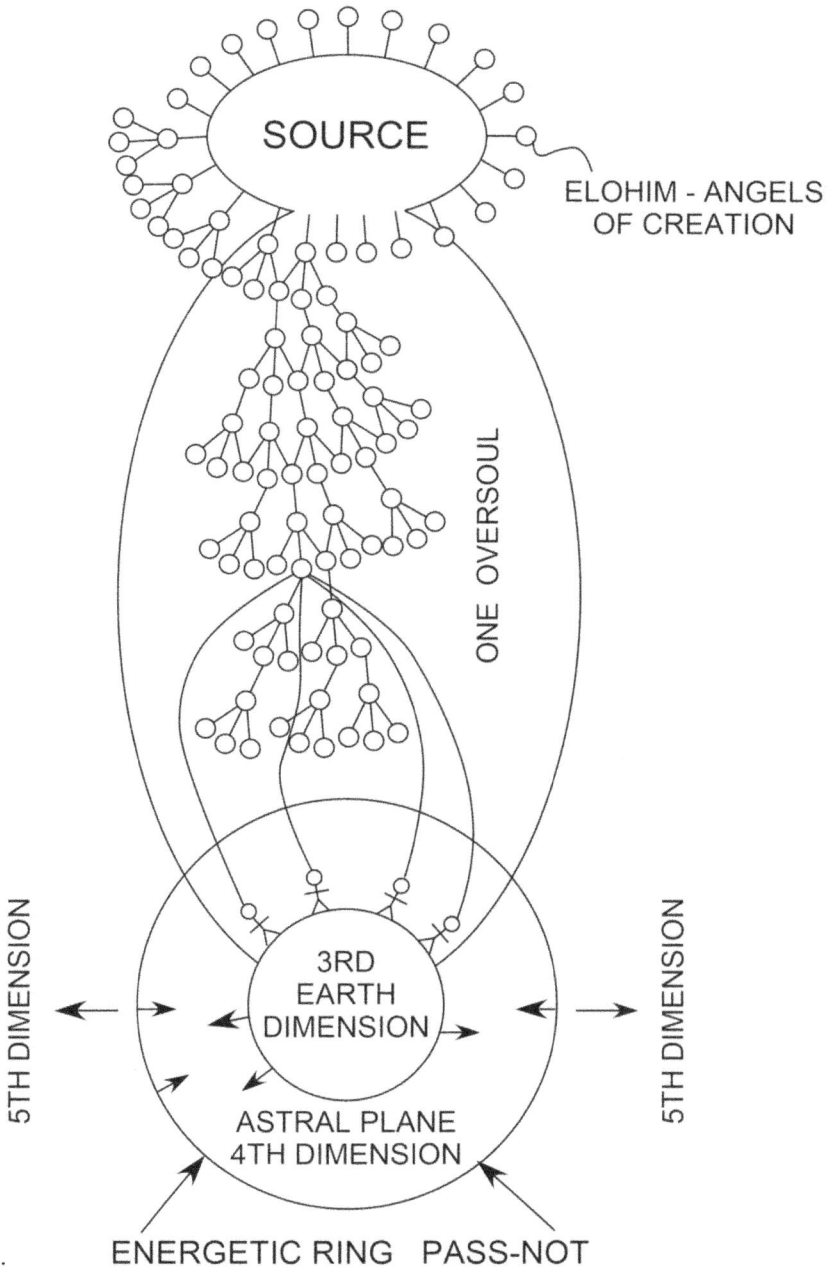

SOURCE

ELOHIM - ANGELS
OF CREATION

ONE OVERSOUL

3RD
EARTH
DIMENSION

ASTRAL PLANE
4TH DIMENSION

5TH DIMENSION

5TH DIMENSION

ENERGETIC RING   PASS-NOT

If you study the diagram, you will also see that you are part of a much larger spiritual family which is operating simultaneously in many different dimensions. The diagram also shows us that the Spiritual Hierarchy, at the time Humans decided we were smart enough to split the atom, chose to install an energetic barrier around Earth, out beyond the Fourth dimension, to keep Humans from negatively affecting the rest of the galaxy and the Universe because splitting an atom creates a chain reaction that could destroy other planets in the Galaxy and Universe. This ring is spiritually referred to as the Ring-Pass-Not. All of the negative thought forms of Humanity are captured in this embryonic sack around the Earth.

The Fourth dimension represents what Christians would call hell. The energy is the energy of red, orange and yellow. Therefore, a Christian mystic entering the Fourth dimension might have perceived it as burning or filled with fire. They would have also seen beings in the Fourth dimension suffering. Beings who die and are addicted to negative behaviors or substances, and have not acquired enough consciousness and energy to make it through the barrier into the Fifth dimension, which Christians would refer to as heaven, are stuck in the Fourth dimension sometimes referred to a purgatory.

God doesn't decide who's going to heaven or hell. Our level of consciousness and energy makes it possible for us to transcend the Fourth dimension (hell) and move on up into another dimension. When we leave our body, we transcend into whatever dimension matches the level of energy and consciousness we have developed during this life. Through thought, intention and raising our vibration we can experience whatever version of heaven we wish to manifest.

Earth as a planet is evolving into the Fifth dimension. We are currently, as a planet and a species, in the middle of the Fourth dimension, in the middle of hell, which we as a species have thus far created by past thoughts. We equally have the ability to create heaven on Earth through our current and future thoughts as a species. The Ring-Pass-Not is occasionally tightened as a person losing weight would tighten their belt. Each time this happens, Earth's time is speeded up. All of the molecules in our bodies and all of the molecules of Earth are speeded up at the exact same frequency, as are the molecules in our watches and clocks so they still reflect twenty-four hours, but it is clear to our feeling nature that time is speeding up. We currently have a eight hour day as compared to the twenty-four hour day we had in the 1950's.

God has been generous and gracious toward Humanity and given us timesaving devices to assist us not to lose our sanity in trying to continue to accomplish everything we have expected of ourselves before time began collapsing. Computers, cell phones, TVs, DVDs, and DVRs, appliances, airplanes and ideas for all manner of electronic devices have been given to inventors.

Even though I've been asked by many people, I've never been told how many Oversouls there are or how many beings make up one Oversoul. I perceive it would be in constant fluctuation.

From my experience, it is not to our highest spiritual growth potential to necessarily ask to be mated to a soul mate (meaning someone from our same Oversoul). Very often, even though there would be a large energy connection, it would not be the most efficient way to expand the interaction between Oversouls and it would not give us the difference that often makes for interesting and growth-producing relationships. There are many beings on the planet with which we can have successful relationships. The success of a relationship does not depend on similarities, but more depends on the level of consciousness of the participants. When seeking a romantic relationship, it is suggested that we look to improving ourselves, which is the best way to attract a partner with admirable qualities.

Often people will reincarnate in groups over and over from the same Oversoul in order to work toward increased spiritual growth. It is, however, normal that we reincarnate not always as the same sex, nor play the same role with other members with whom we reincarnate. A mother in one life may be our child in another life. A partner may later incarnate as a sibling, parent or boss.

After having the Oversoul explained to me by my soul, they later explained the Spiritual Hierarchy and the offices held within it are advanced or ascended souls. Having come from a banking background, you can imagine that I was appalled to learn the Universe is run by a corporation of Beings. My soul quickly pointed out that there was nothing wrong with the idea of corporate structure other than the fact that Humans have not evolved enough to be non-competitive or cooperative. They assured me that the Beings running this Universe have evolved to be non-competitive and are all committed to cooperative effort to evolve Earth and Humanity.

After years of regressing people, I was given access to the Akashic Records and saw how many overlapping lives we would have to clear up. I realized that doing regressions and clearing a couple of lives each session wasn't going to get the job done. I petitioned the Hierarchy to give me a more efficient method, which they did in the Cellular Release of Trauma,

Fear, Judgment and Negative Beliefs CD, which is available through Namaste Enrichment Center.

The first time I regressed someone who showed up on another planet totally freaked me out, and at this point, my soul had to explain the participation and existence of the Intergalactic Federation. As I've said, the soul gives us as much information as we can take in successfully at one time without overload or fearfully freaking out. My spiritual growth, from the limited education of Christianity to Universal Consciousness, has had to be gradual over a forty year period.

One of the most important things I've been taught is to only agree to channel my own Oversoul or Higher Self. It is too easy to get confused about the guidance we receive. Opening ourselves to the Spirit World without any kind of safety discernment is extremely dangerous. I recommend, from some rather horrifying experiences I had in learning this lesson, that in meditation you ask only to communicate with the highest level of your Oversoul, through the vibration of the Cosmic Christ Consciousness, which your physical body can tolerate comfortably. When you make this connection, I've found it to be useful to install, through intention, this Being as your gate keeper, your receptionist if you will. Become so familiar with this vibration that you are always confident of the information coming through. I call this level of my Oversoul, Matthew. You can call yours anything you choose.

Matthew keeps any other entities from approaching me. All Beings who wish to speak with me or through me relay the information through Matthew. There are many astral plane entities that have learned the words of the New Age. They have observed the names of entities we respect such as Sananda (supposedly Jesus' galactic name), Ashtar or Lord Michael. They are very capable of joining together to form a large energy and pretending to be one of these spiritually respected entities in order to "channel" through an unsuspecting person seeking to become a spiritual channel. They can even convince an audience to listen to the channeling and then not only feed off of the energy of the channel, but feed off of the energy of the audience.

By setting your intention to only communicate with your own Oversoul, in the manner described, you set up a protocol that begins to allow you to trust the information you receive. When you first connect with your soul you may only feel energy or see a color or colors. Don't give up. The more you desire the direct communication with your soul, and the more willing you are to be guided by your soul, the faster the connection will be made.

Remember not to ask to hear, not to ask to see, but ask to know the information. Knowing is a higher vibrational way of communicating spiritually than hearing or seeing.

Soul communication and working together with the higher level of yourself progresses you and it energetically through the level of your Oversoul with whom you work. In 1983, when I first made the connection with Matthew and we agreed to begin to work together, he was a Fifth dimensional entity. Through the years, with all the traveling, energy work, teaching, writing, painting, etc we've accomplished together, he has advanced to the Ninth dimension; and my body and consciousness have adjusted to connect to and use Ninth dimensional energy without harm to my body, my emotions or my psyche. I can speak from this level without my voice quivering and without tearing up.

When you come in contact with a person who becomes emotional when they connect to channel, or their voice changes or quivers, it is a sign they have not cleared old emotions from their body; that they are still operating empathically. It is extremely important, now that we are in the midst of the Fourth dimension and so much chaos, for us to cease to operate empathically in favor of operating multi-dimensionally from the level of our soul connection. Being empathic and leaving our emotional body open causes us to be sponges that pick up other people's emotions and thought forms, which cause depression, anxiety and fear. It becomes very detrimental to Human, emotional, spiritual and physical health. Being empathic can be overcome by intention and repeatedly using the grounding process. Use the process on page 83 and 84.

Until a few years ago when we heard the word channel, we thought of a TV channel or a channel of water or electricity or some other substance moving through a conduit or ditch and "to channel" as the act or verb of moving through. Today, especially in the metaphysical or spiritual community, the terminology most often refers to an individual who has made a conscious effort to become aware of energy and other dimensions to the extent that he or she can telepathically communicate with dimensions other than the Third dimension and actively bring information, energy or images from those dimensions. One author defines channeling as, "A process whereby the subject acts as a vehicle for bringing through energy, guidance and wisdom from a source and plane of consciousness that transcends one's logical, conditioned, outer-mind awareness."

I will attempt to use the simplest words possible, or define unfamiliar words, to explain the very complicated subject of channeling. Channeling, as I will reference it in this article, will refer to the process through which information and/or energy is brought from one dimension into another, the communication between a person's conscious mind and a person's Supe-r conscious mind or Oversoul as well as the communication between an embodied entity and a disembodied entity.

THE OVERSOUL AND CHANNELING

Each of us, apparently, has an Oversoul family, a group of souls who operate together to learn and express certain lessons and talents. It is sometimes referred to as simultaneous lives in various dimensions. At some point, an aspect develops enough consciousness and energy that they are able to project a portion of themselves into the Third dimension to experience life for a very specific purpose. In order to determine that purpose, it seems only logical that it would behoove us to communicate with that part of our Oversoul that projected us into this dimension. In my opinion, that is the appropriate reason to want to channel and the logical reason to channel our own Oversoul rather than to just open to channel any Spirit that makes itself available to you. Through communication with your Oversoul, you can then communicate with any Spirit or group mind that your soul deems necessary. You can have access to Universal Intelligence. I recommend you establish a relationship with the highest level of your Oversoul, through the Cosmic Christ Consciousness, that your physical body can tolerate. This entity will then, through invitation, become your "gatekeeper or re-ceptionist" within your Oversoul. This keeps you from being bombarded by every entity that wants to try to speak to and through you. Your gate-keeper can then limit who approaches you and filter information that is not accurate or to your highest good. It also makes it possible for you to trust what you receive from your Oversoul.

There are several kinds of channeling: trance channeling, conscious channeling and automatic or inspired writing. These are the three types I would like to discuss. To trance channel, a person must go into an altered state of consciousness, losing awareness of their body and their surroundings to allow a disembodied entity (a Spirit without a physical body) access to their body and vocal chords. The person agreeing to be the conduit through which the information will come is usually referred to as the channel or the medium.

When I personally began to channel, I had never heard the term "channeling" nor did I know anything at a conscious level about metaphysics or medium ship. In 1979, I went through a series of death experiences; my Mother's death, my Father's remarriage, a divorce, leaving my community and family to move to another city, only to have my fiancé die of a heart attack four days after I arrived to be married and the relinquishment of my children to be raised by their Father while I regained control of my emotions. I was excommunicated from the Episcopal Church by phone by the Bishop of West Texas and the Bishop of Oklahoma for letting a priest who I wasn't married to die in my bed.

I turned inward and repeatedly asked God, "Why me? What have I done wrong?" I kept asking for answers. None seemed to come. One day I went to a bookstore to seek a book on the subject of finding my life's purpose. "Why am I alive?" I kept asking myself. While I was in the bookstore a book entitled *PSYCHIC ENERGY* by Joseph Weed fell off the shelf in front of me. I had never heard of metaphysics and what I had heard about psychics was all negative and nebulous. I denied the book and returned it to the shelf and went to the Psychology, Self-help and Religion section but found no book on how to find your life's purpose. As I was leaving the store, I again passed the OCCULT section of the bookstore and now the book was surrounded by a white moving light. You can imagine how confused I was and amazed. I was sure I was having a nervous breakdown. I had never seen this type of phenomenon before. My curiosity or "something" encouraged me to buy the book, which I did.

I took the book home and said a prayer to God, "If you have a message for me in this book, please put it on one page and I will open the book to that page, read it and expect a message." The page I opened to, gave instructions for meditation to receive inspired or automatic writing. I had never consciously meditated. The article said, "Prayer is talking to God, meditation is listening to God." More than anything else, I wanted to hear God. I wanted to know what God wanted me to do. I wanted to know why I had experienced so many seeming difficulties. Out of frustration and desire to know, I fearfully tried the meditation in the book.

The first time I tried the meditation, I did everything exactly as suggested. I took a shower to symbolically clear my aura, even though I didn't know at that time what an aura was. I took the phone off the hook. I lit a white candle and sat up straight on the couch in a loose fitting robe, with bare feet on the floor, pencil and paper on my lap. As I did the breathing and counting as it was described in the book, I experienced an argument going on inside my head. The words from my left brain were,

"This is not going to work; this is the dumbest thing you have ever done; for God's sake, put the phone on the hook and go get a job." On the right side of my brain were other words, "Through this pen will come the words you need." This was repeated three times when I didn't begin to write. I am not a very patient person so after three repetitions I yelled, "What?" I then realized I was to write what was being telepathically inserted into my mind. The message impressed on the right side encouraged me to keep trying the meditation. After only a few minutes, the encouraging voice overshadowed the discouraging one and began to speak to me of who I really am and why I am here.

I did not receive the information in automatic writing; I received the information in inspired writing. During automatic writing, another entity takes control of your hand and actually writes the message for you. During inspired writing, the words or images are telepathically imparted into your brain and you write the impressions you receive in your mind in your own handwriting. Actually, the information is given as blocks of energy and your brain creates words to explain the energy.

As I stated previously, I had never heard of channeling, automatic writing, inspired writing or metaphysics. My first thought was that I had become schizophrenic, because there were two trains of thought; not two voices, but two trains of thought. I was concerned that I had, through all these traumatic experiences, split into two personalities. My first messages included the suggestion that I try this method of communication for thirty days before making a judgment or giving up. I knew that piece of advice wasn't coming from my conscious mind, because I am not a patient person and would not set myself up to do anything for thirty days. I continued the process daily, sometimes three times a day. The information proved valid and gave me a great deal of hope. I was eventually led to other people who were having similar experiences who could verify that I was not crazy, but had, through my desire to know, tapped into communication with my Higher Self or my Oversoul. You can imagine how relieved I was to find I was sane; not only sane, but on my way to knowing, understanding and working out why I am on the Earth.

My experience did not happen in automatic writing, nor do I recommend automatic writing or trance channeling to you. I do not advocate giving up control of your body to any other entity. I do advocate learning to channel your own Higher Self, Oversoul or God Self through meditation, conscious voice channeling or inspired writing. I advocate learning to channel the Higher Self in order to learn why you are here and how to most effortlessly get on with doing what you came to do. I also recommend it as a way of knowing how to stay healthy. Your Higher Self can tell you what your body needs nutritionally.

The first questions I always ask students are: "Why do you want to channel? Who do you want to talk to? What do you want to find out? What are you going to do with what you learn? Are you willing to talk to just anyone in order to have the experience? Are you willing to discipline yourself to keep your body healthy with the additional energy you will receive? Are you willing to do physical exercise to stay grounded, strengthen the cells of your body by taking mineral supplements if necessary, get regular amounts of sleep, drink eight glasses of water per day?" If they are not sure, I ask them to think about it for a week and get back to me later.

I find that a lot of people want to play around with the idea, which is why they have been drawn to play with Ouija boards or automatic writing. They are not serious. I am here to tell you <u>playing around with spiritual practices and channeling when you aren't serious can be a very dangerous thing</u>, dangerous for you physically, emotionally, mentally and spiritually. If you are not serious, do not begin, do not open up. It is far easier to open up than it is to shut down.

Many of our mental institutions are full of people who are possessed as a result of opening up to astral influences without proper guidance. The astral plane refers to the plane occupied by the recent dead and non-human nature Spirits or "Elementals", they are part of the Angelic Realm, Many people open up prematurely through the use of drugs and alcohol. Some people actually split their consciousness into more than one dimension and find it impossible to reconnect themselves. The astral plane is full of beings that have died in a state of addiction to drugs, alcohol, food, sex, power, money and/or control. Once out of their bodies, they are stuck with their addiction and have no way to act it out or fulfill it without entering another physical body; therefore, it is very easy to become possessed. Suggested reading on this subject: *THE UNQUIET DEAD* by Dr. Edith Fiore, or *WHEN RABBIT HOWLS* by Trudy Chase. Dr. Fiore believes that eighty-five percent of the patients who come to her for psychotherapy are possessed with from one to fifty additional entities.

Ouija boards have been around for a very long time and have a lot of lower vibrational astral energy attached to them. <u>I do not recommend playing with a Ouija board for any reason</u>. A person will normally attract very low vibrational entities by communicating through a Ouija board, especially if they are not trained to seal the room they are in against any negative energies or entities through prayers and invoking only entities of your own Oversoul. Challenge any entity that shows up in your meditation by demanding, "Are you from my own Oversoul?" If the entity is not from your Oversoul break the connection.

Ouija board communication can become addictive or compulsive. People allow themselves to be fascinated by the energy moving the planchette, the information they receive and the unknown origin of the movement, energy and information. Entities can attach themselves to your aura, your physical body or take up residence in your home after being invited by you to speak through a Ouija board. I had a very traumatic experience during my early period of psychic work and warn you not to use a Ouija board from my own personal experience. It disconnected me from my soul. If you feel this has happened to you, break the Ouija board into at least three pieces and burn it to deliberately disconnect yourself from the Spirits you contacted through the board. After burning it, ask to be strongly reconnected only to your own Oversoul.

JUST BECAUSE IT'S CHANNELED, DOESN'T MAKE IT TRUTH!

Students find when they first start coming to class, that various fears begin to surface: fear they will be taken over by some outside energy, fear of the abuse of the power they will gain by their ability to channel, fear communication with their soul will require them to change their habits or lifestyle, fear they will be asked to give up certain relationships, their job, or place of residence, or the unknown. Some fears actually come through from other lifetimes when we have been active channels and have experienced persecution and even death for the use or abuse of this gift. It is a gift, a talent, which can be developed or received from your soul. Most past life fears can be eliminated through energy transfers or hypnosis. Other fears must be overridden by your desire to know, being stronger than your desire to stay the same.

It is very important to clear all of your energy bodies before you open to channel. You have four energy bodies and an etheric field of thought around you, which all hold thought forms. We hold fears, some of which have been projected to us from others, some we brought forward from other lifetimes and all are collected in our auric field. If we do not clear ourselves, we will not bring through accurate information. It would be like making coffee for years with the same filter and wondering why it did not taste good. If you are mentally or emotionally confused, the confusion will be amplified and intensified by the additional energies coming into the body. Fear is not necessary if you become educated before you begin and use the precautions you learn.

You are a spiritual being, a spark of energy or a soul sent out from an Oversoul to inhabit a physical body. That Oversoul wishes to communicate with you. It has waited your entire life for you to remember, to acknowledge its existence and to ask for help. You have aspects of yourself operating in various dimensions, simultaneously.

The beings in the first level of the soul from the Source are what I refer to as the Angels of Creation; we each have an Angelic Presence. You were aspected into the Third dimension from a higher frequency of vibration. Before you left the Oversoul, you had a conference with the Soul and signed a pre-natal agreement to do certain things for the soul, to clear a part of the soul's karma. Karma is the Universal Law of Cause and Effect. You agreed to create certain things, learn certain lessons, teach certain principles to raise the consciousness of Earth, or maybe to create a certain number of vehicles for other souls to inhabit, i.e., to have children.

If you agreed to have children, you also agreed to be responsible for them for a given period of time. This period of time is not arbitrarily eighteen years or twenty-one years, in some cases it is a very few years, in some cases it may be many years. If you try to be totally responsible for these souls, children, beyond the length of time you agreed, you hamper their spiritual growth.

You also set up certain destiny points in this agreement. These destiny points we set up to check our progress or to make sure we have opportunities for certain lessons. First, we choose to be either male or female; we choose the nationality and area of the World where we will be born. We choose our parents. Destiny points are usually events such as marriages, divorces, bankruptcies, graduations, when or if to have children, abortions, accidents, education, career changes and certain trips, or relocations. How we respond to these events when they do occur in our life will let us know the level of our spiritual maturity, how well we have learned our spiritual lessons. All events between these destiny points and, in fact, the points themselves, are controlled by our thoughts. We also plan in what spirit calls "windows of opportunity to leave" the life. Often we leave ourselves more than one time frame from which to possibly exit the body.

You may also have other aspects of your Oversoul in the Third dimension and you may meet them. It is not necessary to know this at a conscious level, but you will have an energetic reaction when you meet another individual from your same Oversoul. These would also be known as soul mates, kindred spirits or soul aspects. They will not necessarily be of the same sex or age group as you. You may ask your soul if a person you know or meet is from your same Oversoul.

Because of the Law of Freewill, which is a gift of God, your Oversoul is not allowed to interfere in your life unless you ask. Negative spirits, lost spirits, spirits who are dead and in the astral plane and do not acknowledge that they are dead, do not honor this Law. I recommend opening only to channel your own Oversoul. If you find after you have opened to your soul that you agreed prior to incarnation to be a public channel, or to be a counselor, your soul will teach you or lead you to someone who can teach you to perform what I refer to as a "conference call" between your Higher Self and the Higher Self of your client or audience, to receive the necessary information.

It is also very important to learn to move through dimensions of the soul and reference only one dimension at a time. There are many different levels and dimensions of the soul.

If you open to your soul and ask for energy or information and do not return energy to the soul through toning, song, creation or prayer, you create unbalanced karma. If you pray and do not receive what you ask for, you can be sure it is untimely or karmically incorrect. The soul always listens; however, it sometimes seems to not answer. Karma is the Universal Law of Cause and Effect. Without these Universal or Spiritual Laws the Universe would be in chaos. These Laws exist and operate whether we are conscious of them or not. Spirits exist whether we acknowledge them or not. The Karmic Board is now available to us 24/7 not just twice a year. We have the right and authority to ask the Karmic Board at these times to balance our own karma, the karma of our family, the Earth and to dissolve the karmic residue left by wars, terrorism and cataclysmic events.

If you are going to channel, I suggest you begin by saying: "I deliberately call upon the energies of the Archangel Michael and the Band of Mercy (a group of Angels who are committed to clearing the Earth of negativity and evil) to remove any negative influences, entities or energies from this room and my body. I request this room to be deliberately sealed on the North, South, East and West against any negative energies or entities. I seal the ceiling and the floor. (There are energies, which are not entities.) I deliberately open myself as a channel for the power of the Holy Spirit and the Cosmic Christ Consciousness level of my own Oversoul."

If at any time you feel agitation, it is good to reuse this invocation. It also works as a prayer of exorcism. You have the ability to exorcise a person or place, but it is a better and safer plan to use the intercession of the Archangel Michael and the Band of Mercy than to get into any confrontations with Spirits. When you discharge a being or negative energy, it is a good idea to replace the space with Light by toning. Whatever tones come through you, intuitively, will be correct.

Toning is a very powerful tool. Each soul has a vibrational sound. I recommend you practice toning intuitively to locate your own personal vibration. When in doubt use the tone of Aum (pronounced OM).

We are in the Fourth dimension, which is full of souls who died violently and were not prepared for death; many are not aware they are dead. They are looking for ways to express themselves. They are looking for bodies to attach themselves to those who are using their drug or behavior of choice that they were using at the time of their death. They are in "hell" with the addiction still present in their body and their only relief comes when they vicariously feed off the body of another using their same addiction. We have the power to assist these beings into the Light through the use of this same prayer. It is important to clear the astral plane of these wayward entities. **Use the grounding process on page 84.**

Once you feel grounded, say something similar to: "I invite the Presence of my Oversoul, Master Guides, Teachers and Angels to be present and receptive to me. I open myself as a channel for the power of the Holy Spirit. I ask that only the highest and purest form of truth be allowed to come through me. I ask for access to the Akashic Record. I ask to receive only that which is to my highest good." (Or the highest good of your client.) If you are reading for someone else, connect from your Oversoul to their Oversoul to receive information for your client from the client's Oversoul and not their energy field, thought forms or emotions.

Begin to be aware of your breath; breathing from your abdomen, allow your breath to become even, the same length of inhale as exhale. Totally relax your body with your spine straight and your bare feet on the floor. Take a deep breath, holding that breath at the point of the mid-brain as you count to yourself silently, three, three, three, and exhale. Take another deep breath, hold it at the point of the mid-brain and count to yourself silently two, two, two and exhale. Taking a third deep breathe, holding it at the point of the mid-brain, repeat to yourself silently one, one, one. Continuing to breathe normally, allowing your body to become more and more deeply relaxed, count backward slowly, silently, ten, nine, eight, seven, six, five, four, three, two, one. Mentally intend to go to a beautiful quiet setting which may be out-of-doors, a temple or a room of your own mental creation. Wait there in a meditative state to receive messages or images. It is good to keep a pencil and paper on your lap to record the images or words, or you may prefer to use a recording device.

Say a prayer of thanksgiving after you have received a message or inspiration or at the end of your meditation, even if you feel you did not receive that which you desired. It may take several attempts before conscious contact is accomplished. The goal is to reach the alpha brain wave level and to stay there during the meditation without dropping into theta or delta. Alpha is where the communication is possible.

If you open to channel large amounts of creative energy and then do not use this energy to create, it can have a negative effect on your physical body and emotions.

If you become spiritually aware and then decide that you are so evolved that you do not need protection or clearing, you are using a similar logic to learning how to drive a sports car and believing you are immune to accidents so you do not put on a seat belt and drive recklessly.

If you pray about an issue and do not listen for an answer of what you are to do actively to cause the miracle, you are not behaving in a spiritually mature manner. Prayer cannot be left to a minister or a priest; it is a personal matter between you and your soul.

It is very important to learn to channel responsibly and in a manner that is healthy for your body and with integrity. Part of your integrity needs to include not tuning in to other people's minds, emotions and soul records indiscriminately, out of curiosity and without their permission.

You need to be a person of integrity if you are going to accept the responsibility of channeling for other people and entering the Akashic Record. If you are a channel and wake up one morning emotionally or physically distressed, it is important not to open to channel for your clients and to reschedule their appointments. You need to decide on your own principles. Will you channel information about the sex of an unborn child, will you tell someone if you see they are approaching death or an accident, or that a loved one is approaching death, that one of their children appears to be on drugs or is having sexual relationships. It is ultimately important to be tactful but honest. Most things can be worded in such a way as to be alluded to, but not blatantly explained, to put a question in the client's mind that he/she may, themselves, question or explore the answers.

Everyone has possible futures depending on their choices. The soul will point out the probable future the client will have if they continue as they currently are thinking and feeling.

We all have access to our own answers within ourselves. We are sometimes too emotionally distraught or unclear or too lazy, to seek these answers and then need a channel we can trust.

Early in your channeling career you may not be granted access to the Akashic records (soul records) until you have proven your integrity and sincerity to the group mind of guides you are working with to bring through information to do readings. If you are reading information only for yourself, you will not normally be given access to any soul records other than your own.

When you first begin to channel, your body may sway, move slightly in circles or shake as the energy begins to move through the body and the body adjusts to it. Once your blockages are removed, the swaying and shaking normally cease. Some people experience tears when connecting to higher energies if their emotional bodies have been damaged.

Once you have opened and asked to talk to your Oversoul, they will send you messages in many ways; TV, radio, music, other people, clouds, symbols, animals, books, magazines and newspapers. When you notice something becoming repetitious in your life, take it seriously. If a word or idea comes several times in a week, research it on Google or at the library, on-line or other sources. You have a responsibility to be active and not to expect everything you need to know will be given to you directly by words in your head. The information is downloaded in an energetic form; your mind and body will then transmit the information to your conscious mind in words, ideas, pictures or feelings.

You may also choose to explore Tarot cards, astrology, numerology, runes, crystals and other methods of divination in addition to direct chan-neling to receive information. Many individuals use these kinds of tools to open to their soul. If you are open and receptive, you could do a runes reading, a tarot reading, meditate to receive inspired writing and then go to an open and clear reader and have a psychic reading and all four should essentially tell you the same or similar information.

Develop discernment; ask your soul for the Gift of Discernment. Dis-cernment is the most practical of all the spiritual gifts; it allows you to know when someone is telling you the truth or a thing you read or hear is the truth. Discernment differentiates between truth and illusion.

It is possible to channel on the phone for another person, because we each have a unique individual voice vibration which is reflective of our soul and is as unique as our fingerprints.

Our ultimate objective in coming to Earth was to remember the possibility of this connection to the soul, seek it, allow it and benefit from it. In allowing more and more connection to the soul aspect that sent us, we can allow this aspect to over light our bodies to become "soul infused personalities." We can allow this communication with soul to happen at all times, not just when we are meditating. To begin to allow the connection during meditation is the first step; the second is to allow it during our sleep state and then to allow it during our constant waking state. Once we have agreed to this soul infusion, our intuition will increase and we virtually will be channeling our lives as they were intended from the level of the soul. In this state, life is more effortless, more enjoyable and more rewarding both for us and for the soul.

Always be cautious, but not fearful, because fear attracts negativity and attracts that which you fear. Use knowledge to overcome fear.

Intend and agree to live in a state of soul awareness, self-awareness. Being aware of how we "feel" at all times is a clue to soul awareness. Negative feelings are a warning sign from the soul that we are out of balance or off track of our goal, the soul's goal through us. Become aware of your heart's desires, because your heart's desires are your soul's desires. We came here to enjoy the process of being Human and to enjoy the beauty and variety of all that is available on the Earth. We can do that most successfully by channeling our own Oversouls.

3.

Choosing the 2 by 4
or the Feather Method

*"If you can learn from hard knocks, you can also
learn from soft touches."*
— **Carolyn Kenmore**

The truth is, nobody escapes this life without encountering some misfortune. The face of misfortune differs widely in appearance, and when it occurs, it stops us in our tracks, forcing us to take notice of the truth of our lives, or we blame someone else for our misfortune. Often, the misfortunes of others seem obvious. We see clearly what they should have done to change their lives. But when the misfortune happens to us, and we are in the midst of it, life seems to be presenting us with a series of cryptic messages. The truth is there have been feather messages, which we have avoided and now we are experiencing the result of a 2 by 4 message.

You know from your own experience changes normally come about gradually. Usually we hang onto our current situations until we can see the bridge that can take us to the next crossing. We ignore the whispers, the feather-like touches of Spirit waiting for more clarity; we wait to know for sure before we proceed. If we wait too long and postpone change, Spirit has no choice but to create an event to force the change, a 2 by 4 event. When this happens we are often forced to make the change abruptly, abandoning all paths of security and reasonableness. It would help if and when these 2 by 4 events take place we could move into the uncharted territory with trust that we are on the verge of a great personal discovery. But usually we are in shock and scare ourselves to death and/or make ourselves miserable.

Spirit is subtle. Usually our intuition, the still, small voice within, is more like a whisper or the touch of a feather. If we ignore the repetitious touches of the feather, the whispers, the next choice the soul has is to give us the message in a more dramatic way. I call this the 2 by 4 method. Our lives take turns for the worse or the better in proportion to how each one of us fulfills or evades our inner calling to change. In opening ourselves to Spirit's influence, our destiny is fulfilled. We, however, resist and want to know exactly "how" is this going to work out? We use excuses for not following the subtle guidance of Spirit, demanding to hear a voice, most often claiming that Spirit doesn't speak to us; we don't hear a voice because Spirit doesn't use a megaphone, Spirit whispers.

If we wait for a burning bush or a big booming voice to point the way or give us proof that this is the right direction, we can wait forever. Spirit gives nudges, feather touches. We are expected to listen, to remain conscious. If we insist on ignoring our intuition, the subtle hunches, the lesson will come with more force and seemingly without warning. Accidents may happen to get our attention if we are ignoring our situation by rushing from one activity to another, never giving ourselves any quiet time to listen to our souls. We may lose the job we are hanging onto, even if we hate it, because we say we don't know what else to do. If we refuse to budge from a relationship, a job, a place we are living and it's spiritually time to move on, we are setting ourselves up for a 2 by 4 experience. I've often tried to ignore my intuition, because it does not compute to my logic.

Often the 2 by 4 comes in the form of the body developing a disease or being involved in an accident. If we need to slow down to listen, the body will give us that opportunity. We create accidents and diseases when our egos are so resistant to change that nothing else will stop us. Some lessons are so unique as to only be learned through illness, especially if we have taken our bodies for granted and pushed ourselves beyond reason. We often prefer to claim ignorance and prefer to think the World has forced this misfortune upon us. Spiritual maturity causes us to begin to ask: "What is this experience trying to teach me?"

Anytime we hear, see or feel something three or more times, especially within a short time period, it's information worthy of our attention. These signs give us feedback about our current belief system, since our thoughts attract mirroring experiences. We are to use these signs to heal beliefs that dishonor us and move us in the direction that our guidance points us.

"There is no blame if we miss the sign the first time or the second or the third, but if we continually ignore what we are given to understand, then surely it will be difficult to see the purpose of the next test. Truth is not delivered on a silver salver but is distilled within from hard work and good observation."
— **Reshad Field**

When a strong creative urge takes us in what appears to be the wrong direction, we have a tendency to believe that urge to be wrong. But oftentimes that urge springs from a positive source – it's just that the vehicle for our creative outlet may be ill suited, or we haven't yet discovered the right time or place to use it. We may go along for months or even years always fighting a part of ourselves, until one day we begin to understand that the many trials we have undergone have had a purpose – they have tested our resolve to commit to a new life.

"A step in the wrong direction is better than staying on the same spot all your life...Once you're moving forward you can correct your course as you go."
— **Maxwell Maltz**

Everything that happens in life is a lesson to be learned. We don't always have to experience the lesson firsthand; however, in order to be able to benefit from it we can learn from observing the experiences of others. In the seed of any seeming tragedy lies the fruit of good fortune.

Signs and omens don't just appear at critical times in our lives, they are always there, but often we are so preoccupied with the nitty-gritty of daily life to notice. And even when we learn to begin to pay attention, it is often difficult to interpret the signs.

How do we tell if our hunches, our intuitions, are genuine or if we are making them up? Usually, in my case, the answer or sign will be something that surprises me and is not something I would "normally" think. If I doubt the sign or message, I move in that direction anyway. Now that's a lie. I don't always, sometimes I argue and ask for clarification. I've learned through the years that my soul likes this, appreciates this. Our souls are there to work with us, not to move us around like pawns on a chessboard. These lives we are living are meant to be co-created between our souls and us. The intuitive messages from our souls are only suggestions not orders.

When you receive an urge, a feeling, a message from the soul, say like the feeling you are to move, change jobs, leave a relationship, it is important to know you have a right to say to your soul: Conditions under which I could do that are, and write out the things you feel would make it possible for you to do that more comfortably. For years, once I was in conscious contact with my soul, I tried to do everything I felt was being suggested. I thought these messages were direct orders from God, from my soul. It took years and coming to a point of emotional, physical and financial exhaustion before the soul explained to me that their messages were only suggestions and that I had a right to argue, bargain or state conditions under which I would attempt to do what was being suggested.

If I've written out what I desire, I can more easily take a leap of faith when the opportunity arises, because I've written out my desires and released them with: I now accept this or something better though the grace of God and to the highest good of all concerned. Therefore, I can trust that this leap of faith is going to take me in the direction of my goal, even though there is no obvious evidence that this is so.

I'm reminded of the Raiders of the Lost Ark movie, Indiana Jones and the Last Crusade. The bridge never appeared until he took the first step into the void. In my case, it always seemed the net didn't appear until I was in midair.

Often when I take a leap of faith, I'm not only opening a door, I'm getting out of the way so that the Universe can perform the next step. Sometimes the message is "wait," which is the hardest one for me. But somehow, by letting things be, and having events take their natural course, we unfetter the invisible forces that direct individual progress—doors open and the way is made clear.

How can we tell when we are in the "flow" and when we are just taking the path of least resistance? If you have written out what you desire your life to be about and what you desire to have happen and you are following: What is the next single thing for me to do or know for me to be in a state of Divine Grace? Then you can be comfortable that the path will have little resistance. If you are just taking the easy way out of a dilemma, without asking if this is the next single thing for me to do to be in a state of Divine Grace, you can be sure that there will be a 2 by 4 event to live through on the path you have chosen.

Life is not a problem to be solved, but a mystery to be lived. If we get this and understand that our life is to be a co-creation, we can enjoy the mystery, somewhat control the 2 by 4 events by watching for the signs of the feathers, and write out what we desire our lives to be about. The more we do this, the easier it becomes to recognize the positive values in what appear to be the negative moments and aspects of our lives. When traffic is stopped and our flow is interrupted, we can begin to realize we are being saved from being involved in an accident by being detained or we can rail at "traffic," which I can assure doesn't give a damn about your schedule. Accepting Divine timing is one of our greatest lessons.

Insight is the ability to accept events and to learn from the process of life, as it unfolds. Hindsight gives us access to seeing the pattern as it has unfolded and clues as to how to avoid the same type of lesson events in the future. Coincidences are by no means meaningless random events, but rather are clues as to how the Universe is organized and we should pay attention to the coincidences or synchronicities in our lives. There truly are no accidents, except the accidents of timing and chance that converge to produce meaningful results in our lives when they are most needed to get our attention.

How different it would be when something bad happens to us instead of asking: "Why me?" we ask, "Who is responsible?" and "It isn't fair!" And "Why did this happen?" And "What kind of God would allow this to happen?" And we voice countless other comments and questions. It is said "true enlightenment occurs when one is able to accept miracles and miseries with equal detachment, knowing, feeling and responding to them as one and the same voyages of the Human Spirit." Higher consciousness, however, does not mean a cessation of physical or emotional pain. Eliminating our expectations of other people can eliminate much emotional pain. Paying attention to our bodies and to our intuition can eliminate much physical pain. Our attitudes control much of what happens in our lives. If we see the World and all that is in it as corrupt, our acts will be based in fear and guilt, but if we see the World and ourselves as positive manifestations of God, based on acceptance, rightness, and a sense of belonging, our general outlook will be brighter and healthier.

We have no time for game playing, no time to put ourselves down, or to entertain thoughts of resentment, hatred, or retaliation. If we participate in these actions we cancel out everything we came to learn about love, compassion and forgiveness. Disappointment is real, but it happens more often when we have unrealistic expectations of others.

Expecting everyone to treat you fairly is like
expecting a lion not to attack you because you are a vegetarian.

Earth is a school. We came here to learn lessons and to remember what we know from other lives. In spiritual growth we go forward, then backward a bit, then forward again. Like everything else we learn, it's as though we have to experience the lesson over and over until we finally own it. Each time we experience the lesson, if we don't resist, if we surrender, we get through it more quickly, more easily. And we are free to go on to the next lesson. There will always be lessons. It is our attitude and resistance that determines how difficult our life is going to be. The more we are able to live in the present moment, the more enlightenment is experienced, without a struggle, without trying, without striving.

Maharishi Mahesh Yogi, guru of Transcendental Meditation, teaches that there are four stages of enlightenment that usually, but not always, develop sequentially: Cosmic Christ Consciousness, God consciousness, unity consciousness and Brahman consciousness. These are experiential states, not easy to describe but, to oversimplify perhaps Cosmic Christ Consciousness refers to that state when one becomes a purely objective observer of all the thoughts and events occurring in one's life, when one is "in the World but not of the world." God consciousness occurs when one becomes acutely and permanently aware of God's presence behind every-thing that is. Unity consciousness is the state in which one's awareness has assimilated total knowledge and knows that the sum of all knowledge is that everything is, literally, One. And lastly, Brahman consciousness is that ultimate state of awareness when one's individuality has disappeared into God's (Brahma's) greater awareness so that one says, "I am God, you are God, all is God."

We are all part of an immense organic being called creation. We all have a destiny to fulfill. We chose this destiny before we came into this in-carnation. Therefore, there is a path each of us is to follow. We do, however, make that path up as we go along, depending on our attitudes, our choices and the intentions we set for ourselves. As breath gives life to the body, so there is a spiritual pulse which throbs through the Human organism, sus-taining the cosmic rhythm and universal harmony, linking every Human with their soul and with each other.

"What you do may seem insignificant, but it's very important that you do it."
— **Mahatma Gandhi**

The path of spiritual growth is littered with the residue of discarded relationships. That does not mean the relationships were wrong or unwise – it simply means they outlived their usefulness. Our paths will take us sometimes together and sometimes apart, but all paths lead us back to ourselves. Each of us is responsible for the image of God we allow to dominate and guide us. The World truly is a cosmic conspiracy created to delight, teach and transform us. If we stay conscious, if we stay in the moment and not in the past or the future there is the possibility for more joy.

There are only three ways to change the direction of our lives for better or worse: crisis, chance and choice. Our lives at this moment are the result of the choices we've made up to this point. We've either paid attention to the feather-like messages of our intuition and made choices in favor of our soul contracts or we've been battered by the 2 by 4 method of crisis to move ourselves in the direction of our original soul intention. Unconscious choice is the way we end up living other people's lives. By not choosing, we allow others to make decisions for us. This leaves us room to blame someone else if we are unhappy. Life is not predestined; it is a result of constant choice. People who have difficulty making decisions do not trust their instincts, their intuition.

> *"Regrets are as personal as fingerprints."*
> **— Margaret Culkin Banning**

A wrong choice is not necessarily a bad choice. Spirit never asks more of us than that we are doing the best we can in the moment. All choices are redeemable. Just because we feel we failed at a relationship doesn't mean it was a failure. We learned many lessons from it. I don't think Spirit asks us to choose between doing what's right and what's wrong so much as to choose between loving and learning. Sometimes it's very difficult to know which choice to make to move toward our destiny, especially if it involves an upheaval in your life and the lives of those you touch. When that happens, it is important to ask ourselves, "What would Love do?" If we do the loving thing we will learn without the 2 by 4. Most of the time when we've made a bad choice we can look back in hindsight and remember that at the deepest intuitive level we knew we should not even be entertaining the thought of this choice. Usually we were running away from something else when we made these choices. It is important to occasionally ask ourselves: If I died tonight what would I regret not having done?

"The past is not only that which happened but also that which could have happened but did not."
— **Tess Gallagher**

Sometimes the feather message comes as what I call divine discontent. You can't put your finger on what's wrong, but you just don't feel right. You know you should be doing something different, but you just can't figure out what it is. It sometimes feels like someone tightening the screws on my mind or emotions, like my actual space is shrinking. The discontent can first begin to show up in our lives as disorder. Often in watching myself allow the disorder, I see that I'm resisting a message that is trying to come through from my soul. If I choose to begin to rectify the order, clarity will come. I may not like the clarity, because obviously I've been avoiding the clarity by allowing the disorder. When the clarity comes I am always left with the choice. What do I do with this knowledge of how I am sabotaging myself? I can walk away from the assignment, but not from the lesson. The lesson will continue to come in as many disguises as is necessary until I learn it. I can continue to ignore it or not act on it and wait for the 2 by 4 version of the message.

When we get the feeling that it is time to let go of something, whether it is a job, relationship, object or desire, it's like a time warning signal that says. "You have ten days left. After that, your soul's going to do it." So the desire to hold on is not going to stop the process of change, your process of growth... you know that it's true. You can heed the signal or wait for the 2 by 4. The only choice seems to be to do it willingly, on our own timetable, which at least gives us advance warning, or do it on destiny's schedule, which is never convenient. Spirit is determined we will learn one way or another. I don't think there is a more frightening feeling in the World than the moment before surrendering to one's destiny when it involves other people.

Every day we experience death. It may be the death of dreams, misconceptions, illusions, enthusiasm, vitality, hope, courage, faith or trust. More often than any of us ever expect life shocks and stuns us with the sudden death of a loved one, a devastating diagnosis, a conversation that begins with the chilling words, "There's something I've got to tell you." These conversations change the direction of our lives ready or not. Life as we knew it is over. But the truth is, if we had stayed conscious, if we had been paying attention to our intuition, our soul, we would have been aware this change was coming and could have prepared ourselves and made choices in favor of ourselves.

People are always blaming their circumstances for what they are. I don't believe in circumstances. The people who get on in this World are the people who get up and look for the circumstances they want, and, if they can't find them, make them.
— **George Bernard Shaw**

We are meant to live through our circumstances and learn from them, not stay stuck in them.

"How many times does Spirit whisper, one, two, three, work with Me? Every day, every hour, probably every minute. But do we hear? Are we listening? Sometimes it's the very frustrations of our stumbling that provide us with the detour we need to get back on track toward our authenticity. Stop limiting Spirit. Work with Divine Intelligence and be grateful that God doesn't think like us."
— **Sarah Ban Breathnach**

Spirit speaks to us in many ways through others, TV, radio, billboards, dreams, feelings, flashes of insight, songs, books, magazines, even license plates. Spirit will use anything available in front of us to get the message to us if we are paying attention. Remember in your own life an "ah ha" moment, when the static cleared and suddenly you were aware of Divine Intervention in your life, suddenly you knew what to do and you knew you weren't alone. You were willing to follow the soul-directed impulse. Sarah Ban Breathnach calls it "the soul's Morse code—the dots and dashes of our daily round, so often dismissed as meaningless – not only connects, but resonates on the deepest level." Remember those times when you feel overwhelmed, confused, and afraid and chances are the fog will lift and you will know your next direction.

We betray ourselves when we stay put even though we know we should push past. When we stumble but don't get up, when we deny what and whom we love. When we let others choose for us; we deny our souls. We live lives other than the ones we came to Earth to live. Watch and feel for the feather messages of your soul, avoid the 2 by 4 lessons and live the loving, creative, joy-filled life you were born to live.

4.

Resonance and Intution

Webster defines "resonance" as vibrating sympathetically in response to vibrations of a particular frequency from another person or object. We are attracted to people and things that vibrate at the same frequency that we do. If we are confused, afraid, anxious, worried, angry, feeling guilty, feeling jealous, feeling judgmental or ill, our frequency of resonance will be low. If we are joyful and happy, our frequency will be high. This is why it is so important to watch what we are thinking and feeling. If we think of disturbing things that are going on in the World rather than being in a state of gratitude for what is going right in our own lives and the World, we lower our resonance and, therefore, lower our resistance to disease and accidents. Fear sets up a barrier that keeps positive things, including healing, from being able to get through to us. Guilt is insidious. Feel guilt for one minute, realize it is a result that you have just done something that is against your own basic moral belief, correct the circumstances to the best of your ability, commit to not repeating the offense, apologize and move on with your life.

In manifesting objects and people into our lives, it is important to remember that what will come to us will match and resonate with our current vibration.

Conscious connection to Spirit creates safety. We are never alone. Our connection to the abiding love of God is not a talisman against calamity, but it is our true protection, even when we feel ourselves in the "valley of the shadow of death." "Be still and know that I AM God."

Be empty of worrying
Think who created thought!
Why do you stay in prison
When the door is so wide open?
Move outside the tangle of fear-thinking.
— Rumi

Believing in things such as the practice of black magic or voodoo makes it possible for anyone practicing these arts to be able to attack us. If we are conscious of our own energy and make an effort to strengthen our own energy field through meditation, controlled breathing, direct soul contact, singing, chanting, praying, gratitude, learning a new skill, being constantly fully present to what we are doing, being in nature to develop feelings of awe and wonder and/or thinking positive thoughts, we are resonating above the frequency of anyone attempting to harm us energetically, mentally or physically.

Several dimensions of reality impinge on us constantly whether we are aware of them or not. The pull of gravity keeps our feet on the planet while the mystery of the dark matter and dark energy of the Universe penetrates every aspect of our inner and outer lives. We also cannot describe or discern the impact of what can neither be seen nor measured. Existing outside of the electromagnetic spectrum, this unknown stuff is a huge part of us, everything around us and everything far away from our planet. Each planet in our system projects energy toward the Earth. Therefore, we are affected astrologically. The phases of the Moon affect our bodies and emotions because our bodies are made primarily of water. If we make an effort to keep our vibrations high, we are less affected by any outside influence that is lower than our own vibration.

It is important to control our own thoughts and to exercise our brains. Exercise, meditation to strengthen soul contact with the body and developing fine motor skills improves the brain's function. Exercise is the number-one activity that promotes the formation of new connections in the brain. Playing physical solitaire with a deck of physical cards improves the brain function, memory and fine motor skills. There are now some video and computer games that have proven to promote brain power; the ones that require complex decision making, skill development and rapt attention. Obviously, the ones involved in shooting and killing do not promote these skills. The capacity to change focus and direction is essential. How we move from exercise to attentiveness, from deep quiet to sensory stimulation, are all ways of building our mental capacity.

It is important to be both relaxed and alert at all times.

The practice of appreciation can be applied to everyday activities and perceived changes in quality of life. Studies with volunteers found that those who focused on gratitude each day, especially by writing down what they were grateful for, reported significantly happier lives. One possible biochemical explanation for these effects is that a heightened state of feeling happy through appreciation causes more dopamine to be produced in the brain that, in turn, activates areas of the brain responsible for conflict resolution and patterns of complex thinking.

"The only real valuable thing is intuition."
— Albert Einstein

Intuition may seem nothing more than an inexplicable hunch or mysterious sense that nudges us toward certain choices or actions. There is some element of mystery to intuition; it can't be completely explained in scientific terms. We can't see intuition on a brain scan, as we can some other neurological functions and states of mind. Scientists haven't identified where intuition lives in the brain—or even if it resides only there. There is much more to intuition than what we don't know.

When we look closely at the intricate mechanisms for communication and interaction between the Brain, Mind, Body and Spirit, we see that intuition is part of an elaborate internal "intelligence operation" in which cells collect, process and disseminate information constantly. Just as our sense of sight allows us to take in our surroundings, our intuitive sense continually monitors our internal and external environments, processes the information and makes it available to us in subtle ways. Intuition may alert us to a shift in circumstance or emotional energy in someone we know, or nudge us in a direction with everyday choices we make. We may follow our intuitive hunches and make highly effective choices in our work. Or we may sense an undiagnosed physical illness. The more attuned we are to our intuitive sense, the more consciously we can receive its messages and act from this deeper awareness.

It is possible to learn to listen for intuition and trust it as an expression of our authentic voice of Mind, Body and Spirit. It is possible to cultivate intuition through simple mindful living—learning to listen closely to life and nature or through meditation, yoga or other physical and spiritual practices or for some people a sudden life crisis—serious illness or loss—brings the inner voice forward with intuitive wisdom, as it did with me.

I have learned through the years how important it is to receive my intuition through direct soul communication rather than staying open with my emotional body and reading others and my environment through my emotional body by being empathic. Remaining empathic and allowing everything that is going on within our galaxy, our Universe and individually with people and the Earth itself can be overwhelming and devastating to our well-being. You can understand more about how to overcome being empathic in favor of being consciously multi-dimensional by checking out information on our blog. (namasteconsciousness.com)

When I first moved back to Oklahoma City after years of travel, I needed to find a psychic chiropractor to help me to take care of my body. After I put the request to my soul in meditation, I began to wake up every day with the song *Row, Row, Row Your Boat* in my head. I didn't understand the message. My next client was a woman I had known for years in Oklahoma City, but I had not seen her for over ten years. I felt intuitively to ask her if she knew of a local psychic chiropractor. Her response was, "Sure do. There's Jacque Rowe, Michael Rowe, Daniel Rowe and Tabetha Rowe, I think Jacque is the more psychic of the four. He works with the Spiritual Hierarchy." I had to laugh at my soul's sense of humor. Intuition isn't always obvious. Sometimes we have to figure out the message or develop a language of symology between our conscious mind and the intuition the soul gives us. We all need to fine-tune the way our intuitive sense processes incoming information and delivers it to us. Deliberately going into an altered state of awareness by controlling our breathing to slow the brain frequency to reach the alpha level of brain wave frequency when we are seeking an intuitive response from our soul is useful.

Reflect on a particularly successful action you took in your life. How much did you rely on your analytical skills? How much did your intuition contribute? Allow yourself to realize and appreciate how you can combine intuition and analysis to make your life more successful.

Listen for these qualities; they can help you to discern between true intuition and impulsive or ego tendencies:

<u>Neutrality</u>: Intuition is impartial. A neutral state of mind allows intuition to emerge freely. When we are pushing for a particular outcome, attached to a result, or grasping at a specific option as the only way, we are unable to hear the deeper inner voice of intuition over the cacophony

of other input. Neutral does not imply that you do not care, but that you trust a higher order to guide you to the most effective outcome. We can create our neutral place of listening in the moment, anywhere, simply by choosing to set aside the noisy voices of intense attachment to outcome for a few moments of quiet reflection and neutrality. Your intuition is on your side; if you are to act effectively in the complexity of circumstance, your actions need to be precise, limited and valuable. Intuitive actions are that.

Physically: More often than not, I feel the nudge of intuition in a physical sense. If I am drawn toward something visually, like a book or an object the soul is interested in my taking home with me, it is almost like the object lights up; not really, but the resonance matches mine and, therefore, I know it's mine. When I first began working with Spirit, when something was important for me to pay attention to, I would get an electrical impulse in my upper right thigh; I thought maybe my veins were breaking, since I had no one to talk with at that time about what was happening. Also, when my soul had a message for me I would get a ringing in my right ear and when the message was coming from the Federation the ringing would be in my left ear. I've evolved to the point where my body resonates with the eighth level of my Oversoul so the messages come in more like knowingness and less like intuition. I highly recommend asking your soul for direct knowingness.

"Easy" is not a sensory experience that necessarily denotes correct intuition. As I've said before, in working with your soul, what is indicated by your intuition may be something you don't want to do or seems too difficult. Remember you have Freewill and can always negotiate with your soul. When an intuitive message suggests something hard or unwanted, write out conditions under which you would attempt what is being suggested. If the conditions begin to be fulfilled by the Universe, you know what is being asked of you is important to the soul or to the overall quality of your life.

Spirituality: One of the most reliable ways to enhance your intuitive knowing is to continue your spiritual practice. In embracing spirituality as a source for intuitive guidance here are three key aspects:

1. How we see ourselves and how we imagine the Universe. How am I in this moment? How do I experience my connection with nature and the flow of all things? Am I acting in accord with my deepest spiritual intuition?

2. Is my meditation vital to my everyday life? Does my meditation grow and change as I develop spiritually? Am I willing to allow my

meditation to shift from duty to delight? How are my meditative experiences informing my intuition?

3. Is my life in the workplace and with my family congruent with my spirituality? Do I cherish the flow of intuitive wisdom in the simplest of daily activities? Have I learned to listen to intuition with ease and grace in all aspects of my life?

Reality Check: Not every nudge is an accurate intuitive message. While the qualities of neutrality, physically and spiritually listening are crucial in developing reliable intuition, it is also appropriate to check out those intuitive calls to action with another person. But ultimately it comes back to one's own deepest discernment as the consequences, good or not so good, of every choice rest on each of us individually. Check out if your intuition involves the presence of compassion and the ability of the action to serve the highest good.

When you are invited to a party, event or a trip I recommend going into meditation and seeing if you can feel yourself being at the event, party or feel yourself at the destination of the trip. Doing this usually gives me a clear indication if the event, party or trip is to my highest good or if the event, party or trip is even going to take place.

In everyday situations, intuitive guidance can lead us to unexpected and rewarding outcomes; missing being involved in accidents, meeting people we haven't seen in a while, meeting new people or just helping to open the door for someone trying to enter the post office with an armload of boxes, because we left home at the exact time the intuition suggested.

The Human body is made up of between 75 and 100 trillion cells. This is a well-organized system, neither random nor scattered, but highly structured and efficient. The cells communicate with each other continually. Adjacent cells send out small tubes, called nanotubes, which exchange information directly, cell by cell. Our cells maintain resonance with each other and the whole body through these extraordinary means.

There is a natural arc from our cells to our brain that informs us of many of the needs of our body: time for lunch, get your hand away from the flame, time to sleep, pay attention to that pain in your knee; these from the unseen world of our cells to the knowable. Yet another arc loops from subtle perception to the mystery of the spiritual dimension.

My sense is that we have a separate intelligence that I call the "body intelligence" that controls what we think of as the automatic functions of the body. The programs or software running this computer can become corrupted by our environment, stress, additives in the body that should not be there, or our habitual negative thought patterns. We have the ability to communicate directly with this body intelligence system through our thoughts and our affirmations to correct glitches in the software programs.

Several forms of physical energy activate our sensory systems: vibration creates sound, which our ears translate into communication; Light transmits images, which we experience as vision. All this information is passed as biochemical packets between brain cells as it shapes our perception of the World.

When we experience frustration, it blocks the access we need to our intuitive knowing. Frustration also occurs when we do not believe ourselves connected to the consciousness of the Universal Source; do not believe ourselves to be a part of God. It is important to believe and to practice the "Presence" of God within us. This "Presence" may appear to us in meditation as colors or shapes, fragrant smells, lovely music, body sensations (heavy or light feelings), temperature changes, tears or emotions. We cannot grasp or command "Presence" to come to us; it is already here within us. Belief, openness and faith help and are useful, but the grace of awareness of ourselves as part of God may bless us at any moment. The good news is that the yearning for that contact with "Presence" opens the door to practices that you can adapt in your own best way.

For each of us there is a true Self, a blessed seed of the most sacred. The connection that comes from the awareness of that Self is gentle, immediate and safe. I do not need to hope that an amulet, a certain mantra, a specific holy site, a church nave, or anything else affords protection. The connection to Self and the Universe is sufficient. Union is a reality and our connection with God is, indeed, a safe path that leads us to communion with all that is.

Substantive spiritual connection involves developing awareness of one's own central core and confidence in one's own true nature as a spiritual being. Almost always, the answers and insights we seek are not conceptual. In other words, we cannot think our way into those answers. It took me a long time to trust that guidance and protection were all around me and that I could move into just the right place, just the right connection, without having to rationalize every step and nuance.

Our personal experience of protection and connection can begin with the way our body works. Cells are specialized and highly adapted to manage particular areas of vulnerability. Skin cells in Humans preserve our outer form and protect us from all sorts of environmental intrusion without being an immovable covering of armor. To do this, skin cells produce keratin, a tough, waterproof protein. The cells responsible for making keratin are called keratinocytes. One attribute of keratinocytes is their ability to enlist other cells for protection when needed. They can mount their own form of immune response to a scratch or cut and can signal a full inflammatory response. The fibers are also waterproof and make the whole skin surface water resistant. Just think what it would be like if your skin were more like a sponge.

Compassion is not a static quality; it leads to action. Compassion can be expressed in words, facial expression, body language and total silence. Often when we visit a sick person we can be a more comforting presence by relaxing in a connected silence with an expression of compassion which will bring comfort to an ailing person. New studies show that the normal Human brain is functionally and structurally organized to sense distress in others. Even the image of someone suffering causes specific neurons in the prefrontal lobe of our brain to fire up, a location that is known to be associated with the impulse to leap to assist. Compassion is not a generalized phenomenon; it is specific to each situation and it is especially engaged when our minds and hearts are most clear. It is quite different in tone from pity, which often leads to stagnation and a long-lasting state of emotional sadness. Compassion looks for an outlet in the form of helping deeds. Compassion, sympathy and empathy are not the same thing. Compassion is combining our energy of passion with another individual. Sympathy lowers us to the energy level of the person suffering. Empathy connects our energy to the energy the other person is feeling. Offering compassion, we are connecting to the energy of the person's soul and raising the vibration of the situation for both ourselves and the suffering person.

5.

From Intellect To Intution

The Human mind is an instrument which we are able to use in two directions. One direction is outward. The mind outwardly registers our contacts with the physical and mental Worlds in which we live, and recognizes emotional and sensory conditions. It is the recorder and correlator of our sensations, of our reactions and of all that is conveyed to it via the five senses and the brain. It is the thought apparatus that is involved in Meditation and which must be trained to add to this first function of the mind an ability to turn in another direction, and to register with equal facility the inner or intangible World. This ability to re-orient itself will enable the mind to register the World of subjective realities, or intuitive perception and of abstract ideas.

Humans are to be a bridge between the material World and the spiritual dimensions. Humans have worked toward exhausting the resources of the material World and have not as yet learned to function in the non-material Worlds. Humans face fear of death, because they have not worked toward being consciously aware of the non-physical reality. It is time for Humans to think about where did we come from and where are we going?

Historically visionary mystics have reported Worlds and realities beyond our physical World, subtle Worlds where they have contacted forces and phenomena that are not of this physical World. It is time, through meditation, for Humans to begin to contact these realms through conscious soul contact. It is time for visionary mystics to become practical mystics; for all Humans to become consciously aware of their souls and the practical knowledge that can be gained from soul contact and contact with Universal Mind through soul contact. All ideas and inspiration come from our souls. The soul's desire is that we make this contact not sporadic or by accident, but controllable and dependable through meditation.

To be spiritual is not the same as being religious. A religious person can become spiritual. A spiritual person is not limited by theology or dogma of any religion or denomination; they are free to contact the Source of all creation, Universal Mind or God, through their own souls without a priest, minister, Pope or intermediary. All manifestations of life are spiritual. Spiritual energies are the cause of every form in nature and Spirit gives each of them their distinguishing characteristics and qualities.

Through the spiritual science of meditation we can gain spiritual knowledge directly from our souls, we can know God. Through the right use of our brains to connect to our Mind we can become consciously aware of these subtler Worlds and energies. We can become aware of our own immortality.

We are taught as children to memorize a huge number and array of facts and to assimilate a vast amount of widely diversified detail and yet we question sometimes whether we have been taught to live more satis-factorily by traditional education. Organized education and psychology both leave out our connection to our souls even though the word "psyche" actually means "soul." We are taught to memorize facts rather than being taught how to think constructively for ourselves.

We are given knowledge, but we are not taught how to turn that knowledge into wisdom. Education produces scholars who have learned and retain a body of facts, but they are not taught the purpose of life, how to build character or how to contact their soul or to do their own thinking. They are not taught to question public opinion.

The word "education" literally means "to lead out of" or "to draw out", which would mean to draw out the inherent instincts and potentialities of the student. Education teaches us to utilize our instincts and intellect for self-preservation in the external World of Human affairs, but not the use of pure reason and the eventual control of the mind to gain intuition or soul contact.

The Essential thing is not information, but understanding, and under-standing can be attained only by personal creative application. Informa-tion is gained from the without to the inside; understanding is a creative process in the opposite direction. A person can know a great deal without understanding anything at all. We are facing a crisis in the educational field by leaving out any spiritual understanding and only presenting infor-mation to be memorized.

The goal of the educational process, applied wholesale and indiscri-mately, is to make us physically fit, mentally alert, to provide a trained memory, controlled reactions, and character, which makes us a social asset and a contributing factor to the body economic, a useful member of society, self-supporting and decent. The current educational systems goal seems to be to standardize Humans.

The experience of things is good as far as it goes. It enables us to move about our World and to manipulate the life-factors with some success. It is possible, however, to get a different feel of one's World if one is able to develop another habit of mind. It is the habit of seeing the invisible in the visible reality; the habit of penetrating surfaces of seeing through things to their initiating cause or source, the evocation of the will-to-know and eventually the will-to-be.

We need to unify the two hemispheres of our brain to link the subjective and objective realms so that we can carry the inspiration and wisdom gained through meditation into our daily lives.

Instinct lies below the threshold of consciousness, so to speak, with the intellect holding the first place in the recognition of Humans and with the intuition lying beyond both of them, and only occasionally making its presence felt in the sudden illuminations and apprehensions of truth. It is possible through meditation and direct soul communication to move from intuition to knowing, which needs to be our goal to penetrate into the realm of the intangible. It may be difficult for the majority of Humans to move out of the realm of the pure analytical critical mind into that of pure reason and intuitive perception, but this is where lies the solutions to what we as Humans have created on Earth. We will be required to utilize our creative imaginations combined with the inspiration coming from our souls to reverse what we have created, since there is a limit to our reasoning ability alone.

Meditation is primarily a self-indicated process of education, calling forth all the powers of the will, basing itself upon the equipment present, but producing at the end a new type, the soul type, with its own internal apparatus and holding within itself again the seeds of still greater unfoldment. Instead of being imposed from without, the new self-educational process wells up from within, and becomes that self-imposed mental discipline of concentration, meditation, and contemplation. This is a system of self mind control which can lead to an inner awareness of a new state of being; it can lead Humans into the Light that is within themselves and to see the Light. Meditation can create a new synthesis of Mind and Soul.

6.

Your Brain is Not Your Mind

Your brain is not your Mind. Your brain is a transmitting and receiving device for your soul, your ego and the Universal Mind. Speed of thought is faster than the speed of Light. The strength that propels your thoughts into the Universe is your intention and your emotions. <u>We attract more of what we think about most of the time</u>. We have a frequency. Everything has a frequency. We attract what matches our vibration. If we think lack, we attract more lack. If we think fear, we attract more fearful situations. If we think we want something, we attract more wanting. If we think we need something, we attract more needing.

When we think, we create neuro pathways in our brains. The longer we hold a thought and the more repetitious the thought, the deeper the rut becomes and the more difficult it is to replace. The good news is the same thing can happen with a positive thought. When we are attempting to learn a new thing: tying our shoes, riding a bike, roller skating, reading and spelling, learning the multiplication table, writing in cursive, cooking, driving a car, playing a musical instrument, typing, learning to play a sport, shaving, putting on makeup or becoming proficient at anything, requires repetition. The repetition creates and deepens the neuro pathway in the brain. Learning to use a computer or a cell phone or programming an electronic device all takes practice. Your computer and your brain are only willing to do what you tell it. Intention and frequency of an action makes it easier to remember.

If we contend, "I have a bad memory" or "I can't seem to remember anything," the brain doesn't make any effort to build a neuro pathway for remembering numbers, people's names and eventually even to remember what you did yesterday. It takes effort to remain conscious. It takes effort to remember. Our brains operate like computers to store information. What we put in is what we can retrieve; however, in our brain's system, the present thoughts can be overridden by the negative thoughts we have stored in our sub-conscious. It takes intention and repetition to replace a negative thought. Negative thoughts support negative actions and habits. Change requires practice and repetition.

If we choose to learn to play the piano, first we read the notes, watch the keyboard, translate the notes to the brain and the brain sends a message to the fingers to play the appropriate notes. After we have done this enough times, the action becomes automatic. Learning to drive a car at first took lots of thought to pay attention to each action. Many of us now do this so automatically we often have no memory of getting ourselves from one place to another.

Learning to type takes repetition. Learning to type faster, or without looking at the keys, takes practice to make the neuro pathways deep enough that the fingers find the keys by themselves. When we learn to do a thing wrong, and keep doing it the same way over and over, it is more difficult to unlearn.

Frequency and the principle that thoughts are things and the Law of Attraction have been kept secret from the masses. If we understand frequency, the Law of Attraction and that our thoughts create our reality, we have the power to become powerful and successful. The people we have allowed to be in authority over us have been invested in not teaching these principles, because people who do not know these principles and do not practice these principles are controllable. Many people know of these principles, but choose to ignore them as reality because it takes effort to stay conscious. It takes effort to change. The leaders want to keep the public ignorant and distracted from thinking positive, not controlling their own thoughts and unaware that what they subject themselves to affects their frequency. This is how they stay in control of the masses. If we do not control our thoughts, emotions and actions, we vibrate at the frequency of the national, and now international, average.

Only recently has the Law of Attraction started to be taught through books, videos and seminars and then only to a very small segment of society. These subjects are not addressed in school. These are subjects that the people in charge do not want the masses to know. And even in the books I've read on these subjects, frequency of your vibration is still not mentioned. <u>You get what you think about most of the time</u>. You get what matches your vibration. If you think fearful thoughts, you get opportunities to feel more fear. If you think lack, you get more lack. If you think about what you don't have, you get more of not having. If you think about what you don't want, you get what you don't want.

It is important to remain teachable for our entire lives. It is important to never believe we know all we need to know. Only when we know a thing well enough to "be" the thing do we really know it. I know people who read these lessons and tell me that they get it or they already know this information. When I look at their lives I know they think they know the information, because they've heard it before, it sounds familiar; but, when I look at their lives, I know the information only made it into their thoughts and not into their actions.

Most of Humanity is operating at the level of unconscious incompetence. They do not know better, so they do not live better. The leaders desire for Humanity to remain at this level, because it makes the masses controllable. If we don't know better, we won't make any effort to be better. Once we become conscious, hear of the Law of Attraction, the principles that thoughts are things, that the frequency of our thoughts and emotions affect what we attract, we are still likely to operate at the level of conscious incompetence because it takes effort to control our thoughts and emotions. But, if we ever decide not to be too lazy to monitor and control our thoughts and emotions, we can begin to operate at the level of conscious competence.

Our goal, however, needs to be to reach a level of unconscious competence; to be so competent at thinking positively, at focusing only on what we desire to experience and create, that we don't even have to consciously think about it. Creating neuro pathways to positive thoughts, to constantly raising our vibrations, to listening to our soul and intuition, becomes automatic when we practice conscious competence repetitiously. We want to automatically think "What is the next single thing for me to do or know for me to be in a state of divine grace?" Our goal is to be so tuned in to our emotions and willingness to follow our intuition that positive action and positive thought become automatic.

Right now, for most of us, negative thinking, seeing what's wrong in all situations, is an ingrained habit. We have many negative habits of thought and action. These neuro pathways are deeply ingrained from our upbringing, from the media and our educational systems. Until we notice these thoughts and make a conscious effort to change them, we will continue to have negative experiences. If we make no effort to monitor and censor our thinking we will not have control of our lives. We will be controlled by what is stored in our sub-conscious, thoughts fed to us by the media and other people.

Everything has a frequency: food, clothing, furniture, cars, supplements, medicine, and electronics. It is important to raise the vibration of any item you bring into your home. It is especially important to raise the vibration of your medications, supplements, food and drink before you ingest them. Holding your supplements and medications in your hands and sending an intention that they are now vibrating at a frequency higher than the vibration of your body is enough. When you cook, think about raising the vibration of the food. Before you eat, place your hands on either side of your plate and drink and intention raising the vibration of your food higher than the vibration of your body. If you are eating at a restaurant, it is even more important, because your food may have been touched and prepared by people who have negative thoughts, hate their job or have very low vibrations from using drugs or alcohol.

If you desire relationships, you will attract people who vibrate at the same frequency at which you are vibrating. You attract people who vibrate at the same rate of the places you hang out and the vibration of your thoughts about yourself and what you deserve. When we disown and discount ourselves—so do others and the World. Self-esteem isn't everything, but without it nothing else matters. Are you mentally and physically too tired to think about, fanaticize something other than then life you have? Would it take too long to start over in some other field of endeavor? Do you believe you are too old or too young? Do you believe you have to have the money first?

The key to loving how you live is in knowing what it is you truly love.
Commit to making your future more beautiful
and more fun than your past.

When you do begin to consciously raise your vibration, things and people may move out of your life, because your vibration may no longer be compatible with your family, current friends or things you have acquired. The good news is that new things and people will come into your life. You will attract people who are more compatible with your frequency. This is not a comforting idea for people who fear change and most people fear change even more than death. It is easy to get stuck in life, but that doesn't make it comfortable. We usually only agree to change when our current situation becomes intolerable.

When you begin to raise your vibration, being around people who are constantly complaining about their lives and are unwilling to change, people who desire to remain victims or martyrs, will be less and less attractive to you. You will have less and less tolerance for listening to negativity. When you are around people who are constantly complaining or negative, it is appropriate to ask them, "How's that working for you?" You have a choice to listen or to remove yourself from the situation. Arguing won't change anyone. You can only change yourself.

I used to listen to my children complain and say, "Poor baby." I finally realized I didn't want my children to be poor and changed my method to asking them what they thought it would take to change their lives and how could I help. One of my children used to respond when I asked how she was with, "I feel like I've been run over by a Mac truck." It took her a year to have it be her reality. Pay attention to what you reply when people ask you how you are.

To know a thing and not do the thing shows our laziness. It is one thing to be ignorant of a concept, but to know how to be conscious and to not be willing to change, comes from fear or laziness. It takes effort and discipline to remain conscious and to be willing to change our thoughts, beliefs and actions.

It is important to begin to listen to our intuition and to our souls rather than to listen or take advice from other people about our lives. It is important to think, "To what frequency am I subjecting myself? What have I been thinking to bring this event into my life? What am I reading? What am I watching? What am I tolerating?"

We have not been told the truth about raising our vibration, or that all things have vibration; we've not been taught that thoughts are things; we've not been taught to set intentions. The reason we've not been taught these principles is that those in charge of teaching have had a goal of keeping the masses weak, ignorant and controllable. When we are ignorant we create less competition; we create fewer waves, show less resistance. People who think they are powerful are usually afraid of people who are self-administered. Being self-administered means believing in yourself and taking guidance from your soul and not from outside sources, being your own authority. It means being your own support system and your own censor. When we are listening outwardly it is more difficult to listen inwardly. You do not need anyone else's approval to be yourself. What are you listening to? What are you reading? What are you watching? What are you believing is possible?

When we don't admit what we are really mad about, we will get mad about every little thing. We get mad inappropriately and at the wrong people. Often we are not willing to admit to ourselves or others what we are really mad about, because to change what is causing us to be really angry would require us to change or for us to leave our current situation, whether that is a job or a relationship. And we are too afraid of change to do it, so we stay and act mad about every other thing. People will annoy us; people will be rude to us, because we are vibrating at a frequency that attracts rudeness, conflict and annoyance.

Being angry with traffic is one way to avoid admitting what you're really angry about. Divine timing in traffic keeps you out of harm's way of an accident you aren't supposed to be involved in. Traffic doesn't care.

Everything we think goes out with the intention, energy frequency and emotion we put behind it. You are affecting the Universe with your thoughts. We did not come to Earth to act small. We came here to be unique and to offer our uniqueness to the World. We did not come to fit in or to behave only in ways that make other people comfortable. We came to be unique, to develop our talents and abilities and to be examples of spiritually directed, fun, successful, healthy lives. We came to be examples, not to be conformists.

From the cowardice that shrinks from new truth, from the laziness that is content with half truths, from the arrogance that thinks it knows all truth—Oh, God of truth, deliver us.

Channeling received 12-29-2011:
"The thought forms of this Human generation repeat the thought forms that have been programmed by schools, parents, clergy and the media. Independent, original thought is rare in Humans at this time, which is why it is necessary to train the Human brain through meditation to relax and receive information from beyond your normal dimensional consciousness. Floods of inspiration from higher consciousness are now waiting to be revealed to those of you who are willing to receive this inspiration.

"We truly respect the effort you have put forth individually and collectively to assist us to accomplish this activation of Earth's grid. The activation will affect all of Humanity at whatever level they are capable of receiving. Ask for assistance from your soul in each endeavor no matter how small or seeming unspiritual the event or activity. No need is too small or too large to be of use to the soul. Consider yourself worthy of assistance. Always expect positive exceptions to be made in your favor."

If you think you can, you're right. If you think you can't you're right.
No time spent in wordless solitude is ever wasted.
The time you enjoy wasting is not wasted time.

We are the heart
We are the hands
We are the voice of Spirit on Earth.
And who we are
And all we do
Is a blessing to the World.
We are a blessing to the World.

GOD = Great Organizing Designer.

7.

Self-Mastery of Mind and Emotions

MEDITATION

The hidden forces of Nature and their modes of manifestation have been known for Ages to contain secret orders, which they have not deemed it wise to heretofore give their knowledge to the World. It is now time for a portion of Humankind to become aware and use this information. It is time for us to understand our relationship to the Universal Mind and how all of Humanity is a manifestation of that great Mind, the cause behind all things.

It is time for us to understand the forces available to us mentally in order for us to play our part successfully in the evolution of Humanity and the Earth. We have historically created God mentally in our image and that God was something distinct and apart from everything else. It is time for us to understand that everything is God and we ourselves are part of God, and that part of us is attempting to operate through these bodies and personalities for the benefit of Earth and beyond. We were originally created to be units (I prefer aspects) of consciousness that remain conscious of our souls who sent us here and to have conscious mental connection to our souls and the Divine Mind of the Creator, also referred to as the Universal Mind. This consciousness, being universal, manifests everywhere not just in this Universe but also beyond. We can become able to communicate with other Universes and species through the use of our Minds.

The Universal Mind consists of two portions, the manifested and the unmanifested. The manifested portion can be apprehended by the Human mind, but that which is unmanifested cannot be apprehended. There is a plus element which is always above and beyond that which is manifested.

The manifestation takes place within the unmanifested and there is always something from within which brings forth the manifested. The manifested portion of the Universal Mind consists of two parts; the visible and the invisible, and yet each of these is but a condition, a part or a diversity of the complete unity of the Universal Consciousness.

Upon the visible plane of manifestation, Divine Mind or Consciousness expresses itself in the two forms which we call force and matter. Physically, we can know very little of either force or matter because this objective World is on the plane of effects. Energetically, matter is either particled or unparticled. The particled portion comes forth from the unparticled as a precipitation of it. By slowing the vibration of the unparticled deliberately with our minds through thought, we can bring vibrations from the unparticled into the particled. This is called manifestation or precipitation. If you place a pan of water outside when the temperature of the atmosphere is below freezing, you will find there is a gradual lowering of the rate of vibration of the atoms which compose the water until there becomes a crystalline formation within the pan. Most of the water in the pan is still fluidic, but there are also these crystalline formations, and we have both particled and unparticled portions in the pan. In a like manner throughout Nature these two forms of matter are forever seen during a period of manifestation or evolution, and it is the particled portion of matter that science has agreed to call atoms. Scientists are now subdividing atoms into smaller and smaller portions. They have as yet not determined the ultimate cause but logically agree there must be an ultimate element which produces the phenomena which we call physical life.

If we look at matter only from a physical point of view, we cannot control it; but if we learn to look at matter spiritually as energy moving faster than we can physically see, we can learn to control it with our minds when our brain frequency is in Alpha, a slower brain wave frequency than our normal brain functions.

We can also accomplish this connection with Universal Consciousness and atoms only at the Alpha level of brain wave frequency. When we are awake, we operate in the Beta level of brain frequency and only through our left brain. The Beta brain wave frequency is from 14-21 waves per second. When we do some forms of meditation, our brain wave frequency moves through Alpha, which operates at 7-14 waves per second, and slows the brain into Theta, which operates at 4-7 waves per second, which is good for relaxation of the body but does not connect us to Universal Consciousness or make it possible for us to remain conscious enough to bring back information from our souls or the Universal Consciousness. When we slow our minds down further, we enter the Delta level of consciousness at 1/2 -4 waves per second and are asleep. During sleep, at various times, we move from one of these levels to another.

Optimally, in order to connect to our souls and to return to Beta with information we have been given by our souls or information we have gained from Universal Consciousness, we need to learn to deliberately hold our focus at the Alpha level of consciousness.

The first time I ever meditated happened because I was so stressed I had damaged my TMJ (Temporal Mandibular Joint) which happens when stress causes us to clinch our teeth or grind our teeth when we are sleeping or even all day. I went to a dentist to get help from the pain. The dentist made me a device to wear while I was sleeping to make it impossible for me to clench my teeth. Two days later I had clenched the device into two pieces. I returned to the dentist to see if he could glue it back together. I didn't laugh, but said I needed something stronger. I needed to retrain my body and mind to relax and he suggested bio-feedback. I asked where to go for this and how much did it cost. He suggested a psychotherapist who offered this service. I thanked him and left, knowing I could not afford the psychotherapist. By the time I arrived home my phone was ringing. It was the dentist. He had gone to his desk to open his mail and found a letter from a California psychotherapist who had just moved to Lubbock and wanted to start her practice by offering free bio-feedback treatments to ten people to prove bio-feedback could alleviate TMJ. He gave me the number and I joined the trial.

The first time I went for the treatment I was so uptight from fear I would not be able to do it right that I was hyperventilating. The woman hooked wires to my fingers and the sides of my head. She then asked me to close my eyes and to mentally think the number three 3 times while visualizing the number. My eyes popped open immediately and I said what kind of number, what size number and what color? She smiled and said any size and color you want, that part is not important. Please close your eyes and begin. She then instructed me to do the same thing with the number two and then the number one and after that to mentally count backward from 10-1 breathing slowly. I was not able to relax during the first session, but fortunately I had nine more sessions and became less tense each time since I now knew what to expect. I began to use the method for relaxing, but knew nothing of connecting to my soul. Later I realized this introduction was orchestrated by my soul.

A few years later in 1979, when I left Lubbock and moved to Oklahoma City, I had experienced several back to back deaths not only of my mother, my marriage, separation from my children and my fiancés death, I turned my life over to God and agreed to do anything, go anywhere, say anything God wanted me to do if God would just speak to me. After this declaration I was, of course, hoping for Charlton's Hesston's voice to speak to me.

EMOTIONS

**Stress in always caused by our not getting our own way
or when things are not going our way.**

We live in a culture very efficient in generating stress, smart phones, unanswered phones and email messages cause stress. They make our bodies and minds feel like urgent tasks that we are failing. Thinking about our stress causes more stress. Feeling that we never have enough time to accomplish all we feel is expected of us or what we would like to do causes us stress.

We all have problems. Focusing on the emotions underlying our problems, which are often related to money, relationships, work, health, shame, blame and guilt, lack of forgiveness, can cause us to feel stress, anger, sadness and frustration. These emotions, unmanaged and unmastered are not only causing us problems they are also creating more stress. If we want to manage our stress, or our lives, we have to manage our emotions

Our stress and our problems both stem from emotions that are being over looked, ignored, denied, misunderstood, suppressed or just poorly handled. Becoming aware of our feelings about what's happening in our lives and admitting them to ourselves is the first step in managing our reactions to what is happening around us and within us. Often the root causes of our problems are:

Overeating	Unrealistic expectations
Relationship conflicts	Obsessions
Money management	Disorder
Substance abuse	Fears
Lack of exercise or lack of sleep	Shame and guilt
Poor Health	Over spending
Debt	Unforgivingness

Master your emotions to transform your life.
Emotion comes after a thought.

It is important to pay attention to our thoughts because thought comes before emotion. Become aware of your habitual thoughts. These habitual thoughts may be the emotions under your stress. If we are not steering our lives we are letting our emotions run us and at some point we will crash. When our emotions are running things, we are operating only from our Emotion Mind and ignoring our Logic Mind. When we are only using our Logic Mind to run our lives and ignoring our feelings we are cold toward everything. When we are in our Wise Mind, we have our heart and mind consciously connected so we can proceed logically with sensitivity to our emotions.

Unfortunately, many males have been taught to ignore their feeling of love, compassion and tenderness and to be strong, which means to be tough and ignore admitting softer feelings even to themselves. Many people find it difficult to keep their hearts open because they fear being emotionally hurt or rejected.

Our wise mind is available when both our minds and hearts are operating together; we are practical, intuitive, flexible, and rule-based to protect our self-interest and take others into account. Living with our minds and hearts open sets us up to make wise choices whether we are purchasing a car, choosing a mate, a home, or going on vacation. Optimally we can operate with our mind and heart open and connected consciously to our soul to have optimal mental, emotional and physical well-being.

The goal is to lessen the knee jerk reactions of our emotions without getting stuck in logic, living in balance with our Heart, Mind and Spirit. Negative behavior patterns are fueled by distressing emotions. It is important that we become aware of what makes us feel angry, rejected, shame or guilty. When we recognize these things within ourselves, we can look at the cause and consider changing some of these by forgiving ourselves or others. Many of us were raised in situations where as children we constantly felt shame, lack of love, rejection or fear, and we have to learn to love ourselves and question is our fear rational and based on what is happening now in our lives. Why do we fear rejection now?

Only we can change our emotions. We can change our emotions even when we cannot change the circumstances. Only we can choose constructive thoughts and behavior patterns. We must learn to change our attitudes; to change what we can and accept, tolerate or cope with what cannot currently be changed without letting it push us into destructive behavior. It is possible to stop resisting and to accept without defeatism. Acceptance is actually awareness of what can and cannot be changed. Attitude is everything.

Mastering our emotions calms our body and physical symptoms and shapes our thought patterns that help us to take productive action rather than uncontrolled reaction. It is important that we identify ingrained habits that are not serving us.

We are encouraged to practice mindfulness by being aware of what we are thinking constantly and aware of what is around us and what is happening around us. Being unconscious of our surroundings and our current thoughts is the path to disaster. Mindfulness keeps us focused on the here and now. There is truly only the now.

Practicing mindfulness of what we are doing as we are doing it improves our memory and our safety. Being mindful of our thoughts, emotions and actions increases our overall ability to be safe and happy.

Learning how emotions work, how to accurately identify and name our emotions and to know what purposes emotions serve allows us to be in charge of our emotions rather than letting them control us.

Sit and feel the emotion and identify it. Being with an emotion gives us a chance to choose to react or respond. Listening to our body's reaction or response to emotion can signal that we need to calm our emotion to relieve negative physical symptoms. Often how we are feeling physically alerts us to how we are feeling emotionally.

Stress is a symptom we cannot get rid of without addressing the underlying issue. We can mask it by using drugs, alcohol, food or sex, but that is only temporary. If we do not face the underlying emotions of why we overeat, focus on sex, want to retreat into solitude we can't change our behavior, but managing emotions takes practice and managing our emotions means treating them with mindful attention and making choices. Everything depends on our learning to control our focus and attention. Autopilot is the opposite of attention. It does not behoove us to live unconsciously or the think habitually.

Rehashing the past or rehearsing the future, wishing, hoping, planning, missing, ruminating, missing, regretting can use up time and mental energy that can be better used to create deliberate intentions for our future.

Mindfulness is really paying attention to things as they are in the present moment both inside and outside us. The practice of mindfulness can become our greatest asset. Attending to one thing at a time, acknowledging, observing and accepting each sensation, experience, thought and feeling as it arises moment to moment and to be aware of our breathing takes practice. It is best not to seek to change anything or to judge it, but to be constantly aware.

To become aware of what we put in our mouth, when we take out our credit card, when we drive or are in traffic, without judgment, but with definite awareness is the goal. Mindfulness can decrease anxiety, depression and distress. If practiced mindfulness becomes an integral part of how we are in the World and how we move through our day.

Focus:
Imagine your attention as a spot light on one point of focus: your breath or sounds around you. If your focus drifts, and it will, gently refocus again on the point you chose. Notice the distracting thought and come back to focus with no judgment about losing focus. It is a chance to practice redirecting your attention. Everyone's thoughts wander.

Observe:
Whatever your focus, your job is to simply notice everything about it: What is it? What is it made of? What is it like? What is it doing? What is happening to it? Whatever it is observe it without judgment, without analyzing, criticizing or evaluating, just observe.

Modern mind is filled with habit thoughts that get in the way of mindfulness. Some are: Thinking about the past or future, multitasking, judging analyzing criticizing or evaluating, having a lack of intention, having a lack of compassion, being in denial. Judgment is our most common distraction. It is important to become aware of when we are judging things as good, bad or ugly. Spend some time during your day noticing how many things you judge and resist the temptation to judge yourself for being judgmental. The goal us just to learn to refocus.

It is a good habit to designate something that happens several times in your day to remind you to be mindful, like a phone ringing or a traffic light.

You are not your emotions, but they do belong to you.

The brain is a physical structure it orchestrates the nervous system in the whole body. Emotions are electrical and chemical signals to the brain. The Mind is consciousness and cognition, as well as emotion. Along with thought, self-awareness and emotion, the mind generates perception, reason, attention, judgment, will, memory, subjective ideas, intention, intellect, imagination, and understanding. The mind is what we think and feel

The prefrontal cortex is located on the outside of the brain and is responsible for regulating emotion. The prefrontal cortex allows us to reach logic and our sub-conscious and thereby our soul.

Emotion is primarily governed by the amygdale, the reptilian part of our brain; it functions as an alarm system, the flight or fight response in the body. It is responsible for our most basic form of stress and produces an oversupply of stress hormones. The amygdale has no way of sorting out an ordinary kind of challenge from a life-threatening emergency so it produces the hormones without understanding the situation. Its goal is survival of the body. It produces the jolts that get us to act now with fear or anger. It is inadequate for handling disappointment,, frustration, annoyance (nonlethal) conflict, and other modern danger zones.

The prefrontal cortex is the center of higher thinking and functions as the brakes to the amygdale's alarm. It can make a choice of how to react. The parts of the brain that start up emotions and the parts of the brain that control emotion are different parts. Understanding the various parts of the experience of emotions is actually the key to slowing down the emotional response enough to control it, rather than it controlling us. Controlling emotion is an excellent idea, because if left unimpeded, the cycle of emotion will start all over again.

The prompting event can create physiological changes or neuro-chemical changes in the brain, or the interpretation of the event can, and those changes can set off another cycle of emotion. Once we learn to identify and tune into the phases of an emotion, rather than to be swept along by a dictatorial amygdale or habitual and unproductive reaction, we will be able to choose how to best respond. Each component of the cycle of emotions offers its own possibilities for intervention.

Our emotions can overtake our thoughts much more easily and quickly than our thoughts can tame our emotions. Taming our emotions can be done, but it takes practice. Every experience of emotion actually has six distinct parts: a prompting event, an interpretation of the event, a physical response, the urge to action, action, after effects.

The prompting event or physical response may be big or small, the interpretation may be almost instantaneous or thoroughly considered the urge to act and the action may be dramatic or subtle, the after effects depend on all of the above. The whole thing can be dramatic or subtle, and each stage may be obvious or difficult to identify. An emotional response can be a onetime thing or it can be reoccurring. Breaking an emotion into component parts makes it easier to get a handle on what can often feel overwhelming.

Sometimes going through a cycle of one emotion can kick off another emotion and then another whole cycle especially in the case of grief because grief can be accumulative. I believe grief is something we don't "get over" it is something we learn to cope with in order to continue our lives without being overwhelmed.

Choose a recent emotional reaction you can reflect upon and write down your answers to the following:

1. Name the emotion you're experiencing.
2. The emotions intensity on a scale of 0 to 10.
3. The trigger or the: who, what, when, where of what happened that started the emotional experience.
4. Your interpretation of the situation as it unfolded.
5. What was going on in your body? What were you feeling physically in the moment? What physical symptoms of emotion did you have?
6. Your action, urges? What did you feel like doing? What did you want to do?
7. What you actually did or said in the situation, be specific.
8. The after effects, do you want to hold on to the emotion? How is it serving you?
9. Does it make you feel alive, justified, regret, sadness?

The objective is to become mindful of your emotions and honest with yourself about the cause within yourself and truthful about why you want to hang onto or replay the scenario or emotion and to become aware of your triggers.

Practice catching yourself in an emotion and name it. Is this what you want to feel? Claim that you are choosing the emotion? Do you enjoy being out of control of your emotions? How does it serve you to be out of control?

Out of control emotions can cause physical reactions such as:

Breathing fast or feeling breathless
Making a fist or clenching of hands
Clenching of jaw
Crying

Diarrhea or vomiting, nausea
Dry mouth
Dizziness
Fast heartbeat
Fatigue, tiredness, low energy
Flushed red or hot face
Feeling cold
Headache
Jitters, loss of appetite or hunger
Pain in chest or gut
Shaking
Slumped posture
Stomach ache
Cramps
Feelings of suffocating
Choking sensation
Sweating
Tight or tense muscles

We can use compassion to transform anger and use breath and mindfulness to gain control of our emotions, but first we need to recognize the cause and examine the reason for our reactions and to admit we are the cause of our emotions without blaming others.

9.

Killer Emotions—Anger

Emotions aren't necessarily good or bad per se; they are beneficial if they and their energy-charges catalyze and compel you to make positive and beneficial life choices. Conversely, emotions, impulses, and urges are poisonous and sabotaging if they and their energy-charges lead you to make self-defeating or self-destructive life choices. In many instances, the emotion of anger can trigger self-sabotaging behavior from the person who feels angry.

Everybody deals with anger at one time or another in their lives. When it is not expressed or processed outwardly, it will be process inwardly, in the body, and usually develops into a disease or dysfunction.

It's not the emotion itself that is positive or poisonous; it's the act that a particular emotion and its energy-charged triggers cause that can be beneficial or self-defeating and self-sabotaging. It is the expressions of the emotion that is, either beneficial, empowering life choice and act or ones that are self-sabotaging.

Emotions can be feelings of love, anger, resentment, jealousy, rage, alienation, betrayal, sadness, hopelessness, neediness and insecurity. Urges can have a more biological basis, such as a need for sex, food, or physical contact. The impulse or compulsion to smoke, drink alcohol, and engage in recreational drugs, *for example*, sometimes has both emotional and physical roots while addiction can be defined as either an actual temporary altering of the brain's chemical balance by virtue of a psychoactive substance (i.e. one that affects the mind) or as a psychological dependency on activities or pursuits such as gambling, work, or even exercise. What's the difference between an emotion, an urge, an impulse, and a compulsion? When does a feeling, a need, or an urge repeat itself so often that that becomes a compulsion or an addiction? These situations are as unique as the people who experience them. What works for one person may not work for another.

The emotion of fear can be one of your greatest impediments to moving forward with your life and growing, however when the oftentimes high voltage energy-charges generated by fear are channeled into your choice making processes, they can be one of the most potent motivating forces to empower you to achieve great things. That's one paradox of fear. Another paradoxical quality of fear is that it can catalyze you to live your life in the most positive way; and yet, it is one of the "lowest" forms of motivational energy.

It is good to examine our lives, feelings and emotions to determine what makes us angry? What make us sad? What do we hate? What do we hate about ourselves? What do we want in our lives? What are we ashamed of? What do we fear? What do we fear losing? What do we do to sabotage ourselves? What does judgment and criticism trigger in us? These questions can often put us in touch with valuable information that leads us to understand some of our strong feelings and emotions.

Anger, whether one's own or someone else's, is never easy to deal with. It is uncomfortable, upsetting, and often painful. Especially difficult is hidden anger, usually left over from childhood, which can have a toxic effect on one's body, emotions, thinking processes, and relationships. Many people suffer from what therapists refer to as a "wounded child."

Resentment is anger that has been buried. Instead of expressing anger in a positive way, we swallow it or feel we don't have a right to be angry, and become resentful and even depressed. The main problem with resentment is that it lodges in the body. In time, if we accumulate enough resentment and anger, it begins to eat away at our organs or joints.

Repressing anger and letting it settle in our bodies is not conducive to good health. We must let these feelings out. How can we handle anger in positive healing ways?

There are several things we can do. Sometimes we can talk with the people we are angry with and release our pent-up emotions that way. Often we do not or cannot talk with the person, so we turn to other methods. We kick and scream into pillows or beat the bed. We can write a hate letter and then burn it. We can scream in our cars. We can hit a punching bag at a gym or even run or play a sport more aggressively.

What might be easier, and more healing, is to meditate and visualize our rage flowing freely out of our bodies. When angered don't overlook the opportunity to communicate with your higher power or your soul. Go within and know there is an answer to your anger and that you will find it. Perhaps the anger you feel is there to remind you that you're not communicating well and in recognizing this you can correct it. There is nothing new or unique about anger. Babies freely express anger. No one escapes the experience. The key is recognizing it for what it is and taking the energy in a healthier direction. We can talk or yell at the person we're angry at by looking in a mirror and talking out loud.

Find a place where you can feel safe and not be disturbed. Look into your own eyes in the mirror. If you cannot, then concentrate on your mouth or nose. See yourself and/or the other person you believe has done you wrong. Remember the moment that made you angry and let yourself feel the anger come through you.

Begin telling this person exactly what you are so angry about. Show all the anger you feel you need to. You should say something like:

I am angry with you because...

I am hurt because you did...

I am so afraid because...

Just get all your feelings out. If you feel like expressing yourself physically then surround yourself with pillows and hit them. Don't be afraid to let your anger take its natural course. You've already kept your feelings bottled up too long. There is no need to feel guilt. Remember they're only thoughts, and these thoughts can serve a purpose by letting themselves loose from your mind and body and allowing you to go on with your life.

When you finish expressing your anger to this person, forgive him/her. Remember, forgiveness is an act for yourself. You are the one who will benefit from it. If you don't then the exercise is a negative affirmation and is not healing for you. There is a difference between releasing and rehashing old angers. You may want to say something like:

OK, that's over. This is in the past.

I release you and let you go. I am safe.

I don't approve of your action, but I understand you were doing the best you could with what you had at the time. I am done with this.

You need to do this exercise several times before you truly feel that you have gotten rid of all your anger. You may also want to work on one anger issue or several. Do what feels right for you.

Another type of anger that needs addressing is "habitual anger." Something happens and you get angry. Something else happens and you get angry again, once more and you keep getting angry. But you never go beyond getting angry. Habitual anger is childish, it is related to always wanting your own way. You will find changes occurring in the quality of your life, wonderful changes that will not only strengthen you, but everyone you know.

Anger was a forbidden emotion as I was growing up in an abusive family. It was the cardinal sin of emotion, punishable by physical punishment, rejection and often by being sent to my room. Not surprisingly, I find myself struggling with my own feelings of anger and especially being around someone who is angry. I fear an angry person's unpredictability. My parents were often angry with each other and fought verbally and eventually physically while I, as a child, cowered under the coffee table not to be hit by flying thrown objects. I never really felt safe.

It took years before I could even admit that I was angry. When I left my parents' home and made my own home, I very deliberately chose a spouse who I thought would never express anger, but of course that did not happen. He took his anger out verbally and by withholding himself and pouting. After I moved to Oklahoma to get married and my fiancé died, I was really angry, but could not admit it and I became very depressed. As my soul would have it I met a man being treated therapeutically for schizophrenia. He had been in therapy for years and recognized my repressed anger. He took me to a building site and insisted that I throw empty beer bottles at a concrete wall and yell and scream and voice how angry I was. It was really therapeutic and I felt strangely safe with him. He had no judgment about my anger. I had always been told by my mother that "ladies don't get angry." This was such a mixed message for me since I observed her on a regular basis scream at my father, hit him and throw objects at him. She only ever whipped my brother and I with a plastic belt. She would also demand we quit crying and say, "If you don't stop crying I will really give you something to cry about."

I was told "anger isn't nice. Nice girls don't get angry." The message I grew to believe was that I should not have emotions. I actually believed that people gave me emotions and that they did not originate with me nor were they a result of anything I did or thought. It took years before I understood that we create emotions from what we think and that we can control them.

I still have trouble expressing my anger other than in writing and still have residual fear of angry people, but have come a long way toward feeling safe. I have learned I cannot change anyone other than myself. Anger can be a powerful fuel for change, but only if the change is self-directed. Now,

I am learning to recognize and admit when I'm angry and use it as a motivation for change. I still often feel I want to change the other person, but now I look deeper into myself and see what the person's behavior or words has triggered from my past experiences with anger.

I now realize I've held generational destructive emotional triggers by being raised by people who had generational destructive emotional triggers.

A minister I went to once for counseling told me that many of us have an accumulation of anger and frustration that began when we were small. This accumulated anger and frustration affects our feelings of self-worth and in many cases keeps us trapped in the past, unable to get on with our lives.

He said, "Most of us love our parents very much, but at the same time we blame them for not having raised us the way we think we should have been raised. Some of us have been physically and/or mentally abused by an individual(s). Maybe some of us were never shown affection and as a result we are unable to receive affection. The list could go on and on, dealing with the issues from our past that haunts us through our sub-conscious on a daily basis."

He developed an exercise that helped me to deal with some of my anger.

Step 1: Be alone and comfortable.

Step 2: Take five or six deep breaths. Breathing in slowly to the count of eight and breathing out slowly, counting backwards to one.

Step 3: In your mind's eye; step out of yourself. Forget that you even exist for the purpose of this exercise.

Step 4: Become the person that you are angry with. Feel what it would have been like to be that person growing up and making their life decisions.

You will find that you are beginning to feel compassion and empathy for your subject. It is impossible to feel anger when you are feeling compassion and empathy.

Complete your list using this exercise and don't forget to include yourself on it. Each of us is doing the best that we are capable of doing at any given point in time. Sometimes we know better, but, we are incapable of doing better because we don't feel it in our gut. I do not excuse the bad things that people do, but I do maintain that if an individual could see an alternative that they believed could work for them, they would try it.

We cannot rationalize our way through anger and frustration. We can only feel our way through it.

When I tried his technique I became more aware of the conditions my parents, especially my mother, grew up in, which were poverty, very little education and that she had to work physically even as a child. She married at sixteen. She must have always been afraid herself and thought that she had only the power she had over her children.

It is not enough to know what we desire to have in our lives. No matter how smart and talented we are, we must also be in control of our emotions, feelings, impulses, compulsions, and urges and their energy charges when we make our life choices and choose how to act and react to have successful, happy, healthy lives. We must learn to know ourselves well enough to have self-control.

10.

How I Learned About the Silva Method

Shortly after I began to communicate with my soul, I began to doubt if what I was receiving was from my soul because many of the messages did not make logical sense to me. (I have since learned that spirit is seldom logical or efficient, in my way of thinking.) I challenged my soul that if what I was receiving was indeed coming from my soul that I needed a concrete sign. The next message indicated, "When you encounter a huge bronze triangle held aloft by three spires of granite you will learn to transcend time and space." Well, I wasn't interested in transcending time and space; I only wanted to make sure I was actually communicating with my soul.

One Friday evening a man I had recently met at a Methodist singles group called and invited me to attend a psychic fair with him the next day. I told him I did not want to have anything to do with anything psychic. He replied that I didn't really understand what it meant to be psychic and that the word psyche actually refers to a person's soul. He dared me to go, so the next morning I met him at a local college to attend the fair. The first session of the fair was a video about Kirlean photography, a way of photographing the energy around a person or object. It was scientific and provable and it got my attention that there might be more to being psychic than fortune telling.

The smell of incense coming from the vendor room was causing my head to stop up and ache so I suggested that before we went through that room that we step outside and get some fresh air. My friend obliged and we went out into the quadrangle of the college. In the middle of the quadrangle was a huge bronze triangle suspended by three huge spires of granite. I almost passed out and wet my pants. Here was concrete proof I was communicating with my soul.

We went into the vendor's room and I picked up brochures for Touch for Health, The Silva Method and The Course in Miracles before I made my apology and left the fair. I was feeling overwhelmed and headachy from the incense. I was catching a flight to Houston that afternoon to visit a friend there who had sent me a ticket. When I entered the airport gift shop, the paperback book rack was right in front of me and there was a copy of *THE SILVA METHOD*. In the early 1980's this was not traditionally the kind of book that would be on display in an airport. I got goose bumps and bought the book. I read it on the plane and the soul indicated that they were interested in my taking the course right away. I was to stay in Houston for a week. After the first two days of my stay I explained to my friend that I really needed to get back to Oklahoma City to get a job. He was a police officer and I did not feel comfortable trying to explain what was happening with the soul messages or that I needed to return home to take *THE SILVA METHOD* immediately. I used the excuse that I needed to get back and find a job. He understood and changed my ticket and took me to the airport.

When I arrived in Oklahoma City I called the number on the Silva flyer and asked how much the class cost and if they took credit cards and when I could take it. The woman who answered said they did take credit cards and the cost was $495 which was going to max out one of my credit cards. She said I would have to wait a month to take the class because they were in the middle of a two weekend class and would not be offering the full class again for a month. I told her that my soul was insisting that I join this particular group and take the class now. I asked if she could teach me what these people had already learned between now and Saturday so I could join this group. She replied that they never taught private classes. I gave her my number and asked her to call me if she changed her mind.

She called back after she had meditated and said she was told to make an exception and to bring everything to my apartment to teach me the first two days of information. I found the class fascinating. It seemed in some ways to expand on the information my soul was giving me through direct communication. It used the same format I had been using from the *Psychic Energy* book my soul had thrown off the shelf for me at the Walden's bookstore. By doing the 3-3-3, 2-2-2, 1-1-1 and ten to one meditations Jose teaches, I was able to get to the Alpha level easily and learned to go inside the bodies of other people to check out their health and to leave my body to travel to other places.

A few weeks later, Jose was going to be in town teaching the Silva Method of Healing and I was asked by my soul to attend, which maxed out my other credit card. I made amazing connections during that class. I met a man who financed the racks for me to expand my greeting card company and paid off my credit cards. I also met a man who became my next husband for a marriage that lasted for nine months. I've used the meditation daily through the years and it has assisted me greatly in expanding my spiritual awareness.

JOSE SILVA - THE BICAMERAL MIND

(Bicameral means using both the right and left brain.)

A few months ago, right after Saint Germain invited me to write the Self-Mastery book with him, Jose Silva came into my meditation and asked that his methods, plus what he has learned since he moved into spirit, be included in the book.

The discovery of the new science of Psychorientology by Jose Silva led to the creation of a mind control program. Psychorientology means (1) to help to reinstate the mind to its own inner world; that is, its own native dimension; (2) to continue to guide, direct and educate its functioning within this dimension; (3) to develop, increase and control its psychic perceptions which comprise those sensations proper to the mind; and (4) to continue this education for further growth and development in psychic applications; by making these applications, the mind learns to use its own field of sensation with at least the same facility with which it presently uses the field of biological sensation. One of the most important discoveries resulting from the research in Psychorientology is subjective communication, the ability of one Mind (The Master Sense) to detect information impressed on another brain at a distance.

He states, "The discovery that Human Intelligence can learn to function with awareness at Alpha and Theta frequencies of the brain will go down in history as the greatest discovery of Humankind. This discovery is sure to change our concepts of Mind, Psychology, Psychiatry, Psychoanalysis and Hypnoanalysis and of the Sub-conscious. Practitioners of meditation who gain alpha and theta levels of brain frequency can sense information by means other than through the five physical senses. At these frequencies it is possible to make stronger impressions on one's brain cells and thereby retain the information they have read or heard."

Jose learned and taught, "This discovery indicates that the Human brain, mind and intelligence functioning at these levels have tremendous problem solving potential; it also indicates that Human intelligence is not only capable of sensing information impressed on its own brain, but also appears to be capable of sensing information on other brains at a distance. This kind of sensing of information when awareness is functioning at lower frequencies of brain is called subjective communication."

He also taught us, "The brain is like a filing cabinet; information has been stored in it since the first Human being set foot on this planet, functioning at a primitive level of animal life. This information has been passed on from father to son in many ways, including the genetic means of transmission."

The most important thing his method taught us was the technique to get into the alpha state of consciousness. Everything else he taught was a consequence of connecting to the right hemisphere of our brains by turning our eyes upward and using the counting technique to reach alpha: Take a breath, hold it at midbrain to activate the pituitary and pineal glands, counting 3-3-3 and exhale; take another breath, hold at mid brain and count 2-2-2 and exhale; take a third breath and hold it at the midbrain, counting 1-1-1 and exhale; now, breathing normally, mentally count backward from ten to one. If we keep our thumb and first two fingers of both hands together as we go into the meditation repeatedly it trains our brains that we want to go to alpha. When we put our fingers together in this way even when we are not in meditation our brain would go to the frequency of alpha.

Coming out of meditation:

The Silva Method for coming out of meditation is to say mentally, "I am going to count from 1 to 5. When I reach 5, I will open my eyes, feeling wide awake, feeling fine and in perfect health, better than before...1, 2, 3, 4, 5; eyes open, wide awake, better than before. And this is so.

Jose mentioned, "Scientists have been studying the brain electronically. In the waking state, the electrical pulsations of the brain are at their highest, over 14 cycles per second. In deep slumber, these pulsations are slowest, around 0.5 to 3.5 per second. Brain wave researchers have divided these pulsations into four frequency bands, from lowest to highest: Delta, Theta, Alpha and Beta. The five physical senses: Touch, Taste, Smell,

Hearing and especially Seeing are associated with the Beta level of brain functioning. Apparently all information impressed through our physical senses is filed in some sub-compartment within Beta."

In his research and teaching, Jose learned to project and to teach that a Human can learn to project his Master Sense (The Mind) to the Alpha-producing part of the brain and function from that perspective with awareness. The Alpha producing part of the brain is a dimension within itself, apparently a dimension that has been neglected in Humanity's evolution. The Alpha dimension has a complete set of sensing faculties as the Beta dimension does. Since we have not been using the Alpha dimension with awareness, we now need to orient the Psyche (Mind). With development of mind control proficiency a person can sense, whenever there is a need, information not available through the five physical senses.

In Jose's teaching, he recommended that we imagine and create a laboratory where we would mentally take the etheric body of the people we were working on to send healing energy. We were to include in the library golden oil as well as many devices we imagined that could assist us with the healings. He taught us to separate our consciousness from our body to check out the body of a person at a distance to ascertain any abnormalities in the person's body and to use these substances and devices mentally to assist the person to heal themselves.

Jose recommended visualization. He now knows that to visualize one has to lower their vibration to the Third or Fourth Dimension and that it is better to keep our vibration high and to imagine rather than to attempt to visualize. The ability to hear spiritually would also require us to lower our vibration to the Fourth or lowest part of the Fifth dimension. It is better to ask our soul for knowingness and to keep our vibration high in order to receive the information from our soul through telepathy rather than to demand a voice. When we receive knowingness, it is as clear and complete as if we saw, heard and felt the situation or object.

He taught us how to separate our consciousness to observe events happening in other Earth locations. He now wants to include how to separate our consciousness so we can take our consciousness and etheric bodies into other dimensions by the same method.

He taught us to invite guides into our laboratory to help us with the diagnosis and healing. I invited Saint Frances and Joan of Arc. To my surprise they had never met each other and when they first came into my laboratory they went to a corner and enjoyed meeting each other and conversing and completely ignored me. I later learned that it was better and more useful to invite other higher levels of my Oversoul to be my guides in my laboratory. Jose now recommends that our guides be beings only from our own Oversouls.

He also recognizes that he did not include or teach psychic protection. He now agrees with my soul about how important grounding and protection are by sealing the room we are in on the North, South, East and West, the ceiling and the floor from any negative influence, energy or entity before we meditate and before we leave our bodies to travel into other dimensions or areas.

He taught us that we could retrain our sub-conscious minds while we were in alpha to correct habits and replace self-sabotaging beliefs by inserting new beliefs.

GROUNDING PROCESS

This process will take about two minutes each morning and begins to create a cocoon or barrier of protection between yourself and other people and other dimensions, other than the information coming directly to you from your soul. It removes the static. It also protects you from astral plane interference and possible possession by astral entities. If you catch yourself behaving empathically during the day, stop and redo the process.

In a standing position, take a deep breath and focus on the soles of your feet. As you exhale, deliberately intention beams of energy about the size of fluorescent light bulbs (or Luke Skywalker's light saber) going from the soles of your feet into the central core energy of the Mother Earth, or see yourself as a tree with roots going into the center of the Earth.

Take another deep breath and, as you exhale, focus on your heart, deliberately opening your heart in love and appreciation to the Earth, to your physical body and to your Oversoul (God, the sky, the Universal Life Force Energy, or whatever vision works for you.)

Take another deep breath and, as you exhale, open the crown of your head and have the intention of deliberately sending a beam of energy, about the size of a fluorescent light tube, from your heart, through your high heart, through the point of your mid-brain into the Cosmic Christ Consciousness level of your own Oversoul. (Send the beam of energy to the Sun or to God, or whatever image works for you.)

Continuing to breathe deeply, begin to swing your arms gently at your sides to and fro, back to front, as if you are pumping energy up from the

Earth. After about one minute, change your focus to above your head and begin to pump energy down from your Oversoul. As you pump, you want to also intention pumping up balloons of energy around your body. The first balloon is white and is about twelve feet in all directions from the body; the second balloon, which is pink and inside the first, is about eight feet in all directions from the body; the third balloon is purple and is about four feet in all directions from the body. The purple balloon becomes your personal energy supply, impenetrable by others. The white and pink energy fields are excess energy, which you can afford to share with others. Very few people on the planet are spiritually adept enough to penetrate your personal energy field if you use this system.

He also did not, but now does, recommend calling forth the Violet Flame of Transmutation, the use of the Rays or calling forth the Blue Light of Protection which he now highly recommends.

One of the things taught in the Silva Method that I have found very useful is the glass of water technique. When we have a question we are curious about or struggling with we can drink one half of a glass of water and notify our cells to search for the answer and to make the answer available to us within 24 hours. Upon awakening the next morning, we drink the second half of the water and go about our day mindful of any way the Universe can get the information to us. This method is amazing and has served me greatly.

Another similar method that I use, which was not in Jose's teaching, is to get help to find objects I have misplaced. I decree, "Saint Anthony, Saint Anthony, Saint Anthony, please come around, something is lost and must be found." After the decree my soul has taught me to make the sound HUUUUU. This usually works immediately, but sometimes the answer comes within the next 24 hours. This is especially helpful since things seem to be slipping from one dimension into another. I can look for a thing and it is not where I usually place it so I look in many other places and still can't find it. I do the ritual and go on about my business. A few hours or days later I look in the normal place where I usually place the thing and it is now there. This situation can be very annoying if we do not understand what is happening and even if we do understand.

The ability to leave my body to check on my children has been especially useful to me during the years I travelled and they lived with their father in Texas. They were not particularly happy that I could do it and know what was happening with them. When I would call them to ask how they were they would usually reply, "Fine," rather than telling me the truth, so it eased my mind and filled in the blanks left by their lack of communication.

MY PERSONAL MORNING MEDITATION

This meditation is a result of using the Silva Meditation
plus other things that my soul has suggested.

I deliberately seal this room on the north, south, east and west, the ceiling and the floor from any negative energy or entity. I ground myself into the magnetic energy at the core of the Earth to be stable and to strengthen the iron in my blood.

I call forth the blue light of protection for myself, Muffin, my home, car and my family. I ask to extend this protective bubble of blue light of protection from Guthrie to Norman and from Shawnee to El Reno; protection from damaging high winds, excessive rain, flooding, hail, excessive snow and ice, fire, tornadoes, earthquakes, theft, terrorism and violence.

I ask my body intelligence to normalize all of my glands to produce exactly the amount of hormones and substances my body needs to perform perfectly, no more and no less than each gland needs to produce. I ask to dissipate, dissipate, dissipate any static electricity collected in my body and to perfectly polarize my body between the north and south poles.

I open my heart in gratitude for my body, my Oversoul, my I Am Presence, my Holy Christ self, the Earth, all the animals, plants, minerals, water, fire, air and ethers, the Spiritual Hierarchy, the Intergalactic Federation, all the Angelic Realm, the Sun and the Moon, the Creator God of all Universes.

I ask for the Violet Flame of Transmutation to flow through the cells of my body, my conscious and sub-conscious minds to remove all limiting beliefs, doubts, fears, judgments, negativity, jealousy and anger. I ask that all the cells of my body be healed and transformed to perfection.

I send a beam of energy from my heart, through my high heart and my mid-brain and into all levels of my Oversoul, my I AM Presence, my Holy Christ self, and into the Ascended Master's octave of Light.

I give my I AM Presence and Holy Christ Self dominion over my body, my thoughts, emotions and actions. I take a deep breath, hold it at the point of my mid-brain and count 3, 3, 3 and exhale. I take another deep breath, hold it at the mid-brain and count 2, 2, 2 and exhale. I take another deep breath, hold it at the mid-brain and count 1, 1, 1 and exhale. I count backward from 10 to one and sit quietly and wait for the telepathic messages from my soul about what is the next single thing for me to do or know for me to be in a state of Divine Grace?

When you catch yourself having a negative thought, as quickly as possible voice the word cancel, cancel, cancel three times to keep the thought from registering and logging into your sub-conscious mind.

I personally consider my soul having me take Silva courses to be some of the greatest gifts I've given myself in this lifetime.

11.

Self-Mastery of Divine Energy
For Manifestation

We are in a time period in history and evolution that the Hindis refer to as the Kali Yuga which they consider to be the dark days before the Golden Age. Enlightenment and manifestation have been taught since ancient times, but only in this Age are they becoming available to the general public rather than being occult or "hidden," which that word actually means. They've only been taught in Mystery Schools and in secret sects or secret societies to a small group of people in each Age. Now is the time for us to have this information to use and practice it for our own betterment and the betterment of all Humanity and Earth. To move out of our old lives and into our new lives, we need Divine energy as well as to understand and use spiritual tools. Divine help is available in the form of our souls, the Ascended Masters and Angels. We can have a lot of theories and read a lot about Spiritual philosophy and spiritual growth, but if we do not <u>practice</u> spiritual meditation, spiritual thinking and spiritual action, theory is useless.

According to Sri Siva, a saint from India who came to America to teach about the Age of Miracles which he says began June 14, 2002, we are now in a position to create miracles. We are the messiah we have waited for. The time is now for us to accept our own divinity. The most important change that will be taking place on the Earth now will be within our minds and the way we think. We are living in the most auspicious time in the history of the Universe. At this time, right now, tremendous spiritual energy is available for us to change our lives into the life of our dreams. It is also a time of unprecedented opportunity for Humankind to advance its spiritual evolution faster and farther than ever before in history.

Right now, the Divine is pouring Light into our hearts and minds to rebuild a higher, happier consciousness to bring in the promised new Golden Age.

"Philosophy never bakes bread, which is to say philosophy is not practical."

We are here to become practical mystics; to live spiritual lives that also help us with our practical, physical dimensional lives. Manifestation rituals are not just about bringing physical stuff into our lives, but are about enhancing our spirituality and cultivating our relationship with the Divine.

It is not a time for us to withdraw from worldly responsibilities to be spiritual, but a time for us to do everything we do with spiritual intent and energy. Running away from our current lives to be monks, nuns, or recluses is not practical or relevant for current contemporary civilization. Destruction of the ego does not mean losing the purpose of one's life. We are not to destroy our egos, but to tame the ego into cooperation with our souls.

It is important to be really clear about our goals, our personal goals and our planetary goals. We need to have the resolve to achieve our goals. Often people do not manifest because they do not remember what they want to manifest. Stay conscious of your goals by writing them down. When we were in the Third dimension, we could wish a thing, hope a thing, pray for a thing, but we are now in the Fourth dimension and the rules of the Fourth dimension require that we write out our goals so that our souls and Angels have permission to then help us to achieve our goals.

"To run away from the World is to run away from God." Sri Siva

Manifestation happens as a result of desire, belief and expectancy. To write out your desires I recommend using the form Spirit has given us. At the top of each page write: "I desire, intend, deserve now gratefully accept..." and then describe the items or desires. At the bottom of the page, because we seldom think big enough according to our souls, I have found it to be a good idea to write: "I now accept this or something better, through the grace of God and to the highest good of all concerned."

You will notice that in each cause I have used the word "now." You will also notice that I do not use the words "want" or "need." Our sub-conscious minds take us literally and it is the sub-conscious mind that brings the manifestation. Using either of these words causes our sub-conscious to believe we want to stay in a state of wanting or needing rather than receiving. I use now because, literally, now is all there is. Past and future do not exist except in our minds.

What we think about is what we get. If we think we lack something, whether it is love, friends, money or health, we will stay in a state of lack.

In general, spiritual people shy away from money. This is a historic truth partially because segments of the *Bible* and other religious teachings told us how being spiritual and having money was a sin or not truly spiritual. Now is the time for spiritual people to change our negative attitude towards money and material life and for all people to stop thinking "lack." The World is abundant and everything we need or desire is available to us if we think correctly.

I heard a conversation between Maharishi, the leader of the transcendental meditation movement, and Deepak Chopra. Maharishi was telling Deepak of his intention to build meditation temples all over the World. Deepak asked Maharishi, "Where is the money going to come from to accomplish your dream?" The Maharishi replied, "From where ever it is now." This thought created light bulbs to go on in my head. I had not thought in terms of money already existing everywhere and that all I had to do was mentally move it to where I desired it to be. This idea alone has changed my prosperity.

Karma is one's destiny. There is a way out of karma. The literal meaning of karma is action. Thinking is action. Everything we think creates vibrations and leaves impressions. The Buddha said that one's whole life consists of one's thoughts. This is the best definition of karma I have ever found. We caused the life that we are living now. We may not like the reality we have created, but at the moment we created it we thought that it was the best that could be accomplished. That's why we created it. Nobody else is responsible for our creating. When we did this we did not know any better. Now we can be deliberate in our thinking and in our manifestations of a new life.

Our souls are just a collection of electrical energy. Through breath awareness and intention, we can access our soul; we can see and understand our future possibilities. Once we recognize that what we are thinking is creating future possibilities, we can diffuse a lot of our desires that are not life supporting; things we have created out of our ignorance of the Law that thoughts are things.

There are two kinds of reality. One is a spiritual reality and another is a material reality. It is possible to change, but it requires energy to wake up and diffuse our karma by changing our thoughts. Once a thing is physical it is more difficult to change. To change a thought before it becomes physical is easier. It is easier to realize I am thinking about having a candy bar than it is to take the ten pounds off my abdomen. When we begin to pay attention to our thoughts and cancel the ones we do not wish to have materialize by saying "cancel, cancel, cancel," life gets smoother. We can change our destiny by making a decision to change our lives by becoming alert to what we are thinking and by being aware of our bodies and our surroundings at all times. It requires a tremendous amount of spiritual energy to do things better, but it will change your life for the better.

It is challenging to remain conscious at all times. We are used to being able to do things unconsciously, from memory; we love to take a break and forget ourselves and our body. Try being conscious of your breathing for an hour without missing one breath. The breath and the mind are related. Attention will diffuse karma. When we are attentive, things cannot get overlooked. We can stop negative things from happening when we pay attention. Accidents happen when we stop paying attention. Attention and care are synonymous. What we need is care, more attention. When we bring more attention, more consciousness into our minds, we become more alert and negative things happen less and less. Living without karma is produced by awareness.

To meditate means to think deeply. In Sanskrit, the word for meditation means thinking deeply. It doesn't mean keeping your eyes closed or sitting in the lotus position. Anything that we deeply, deeply think is meditation. Even when we are thinking constantly about something we want to manifest, we are in meditation. Meditation can happen while we are doing any repetitive action. What we want to develop is constant awareness of ourselves, our bodies and what is happening around us.

We are infinite. We have incorrectly defined ourselves. We have limited our thinking about ourselves to our body-identity. When we teach ourselves, with the help of our souls, how to leave the body and take our consciousness with us, we can become more aware of our true selves. Some people do this as an escape mechanism and are hardly present for their physical lives; they zone out. What is important for us to accomplish is to learn how to slow our brain frequency while remaining consciously aware of what is happening in our lives and in other dimensions of ourselves simultaneously.

Sri Siva says that if we want to change our minds we must change the sounds in our consciousness, because our minds have a sound pattern. Our unconscious has a sound pattern. He contends that if we change these patterns we will find ourselves manifesting the life of our dreams, our destiny. He teaches that mantras, combined with intention and attention, can create miracles in our lives.

Everything that happens in our life depends upon how we spend our thought energy. We are the product of our thoughts.

Everything starts with our thinking process so we should be constantly absorbed in looking at what we are thinking. Whatever we think becomes a reality in the invisible space-time complex of our soul, and then it manifests after an appropriate lapse of time. Everything is first created by our mind. So we need to become very, very responsible in controlling our mind, because everything we think is going to manifest as our reality.

Most of the thoughts we have, approximately 99% of them, are devoted to this World. We think about our survival, relationships, money, our health, our jobs, our fears, our doubts, our responsibilities, our problems. Once we begin to observe our thoughts, we can become aware that we can go with them or to regulate them. Meditation and identifying our thoughts can liberate us from our habitual and negative thinking. It is important to realize that it is very difficult to stay away from worldly thoughts because we live in a material plane which makes constant demands on us to stay focused on our day-to-day survival.

These thoughts about the World are almost an involuntary process. It seems an autonomous process, but it is not. The moment we begin to evaluate our own thinking process, we will understand that we really do have a choice to either think worldly thoughts or go to the spiritual plane and think thoughts about enlightenment and higher states of consciousness. How can we deal with Worldly thoughts? It is not a good idea to get rid of them. The best we can do is to choose the worldly thoughts we want to think and to stick with them. Focus only on the thoughts you desire to have manifest.

When we wake up in the morning, there are a number of obligations for the day that we need to think about; however, it is also a good idea to come up with a set of thoughts that we want to think about on a daily basis, thoughts that are very productive. We need to think about finances and other important considerations, but it is so important that we think these thoughts positively and not with fear and negativity. If we are concerned about money, rather than to think about the lack, we can think of a sum of money that is more than we are now attracting to ourselves. This will give us a new consciousness. We usually do not know currently how to make that money right away or how that money could come to us. It is important not to think about the how.

We need to select an amount that can give us a reasonably good life so that we do not have to work until the end of our life on the Earth plane. Once we have the money in our mind, we can pray to God or our soul. Next we should breathe deeply and focus to bring more Divine energy into our body and minds. The Divine, our souls, desires to assist us to manifest. It is best if we do not attempt to figure out how this could happen. If we meditate, our soul will give us, in baby steps, our part as the next thing for us to do or know to be in a state of Divine Grace. This is our part; the how is God's part.

I constantly use this question in staying in contact with my soul to always know the next place to be, when to get there and what to take with me and live in an intention to let my soul speak through me when necessary. What is the next single thing for me to do or know for me to be in a state of Divine Grace?

We need to think about our desires for health, physical fitness and wealth without obsessing. Setting aside 15 to 20 minutes a day to think positively about our desires and then releasing them for the Divine to work on them is the best method. It causes us to begin to take control of our worldly thoughts.

We are the hosts of our thoughts. If we become aware of one that we do not want to manifest, we can dismiss it. Thought control is an essential part of manifesting a life of prosperity, health and enlightenment. It is important for us to consciously substitute a positive dream for a negative dream because, if we can dream it, we can have it. The problem is that it is impossible for us to hold onto the same thought for an extended period of time. This is why it is so important for us to learn to focus. Manifesting is just dreaming. There is a very close relationship between getting rich in a dream and getting rich in reality. Both are dreams. We think that only the dream at night is unreal. But the reality we experience in the waking state is also a dream. When we realize this we are enlightened. This is why it is so important that we teach ourselves to dream in the waking-state reality, the Alpha state. Dreaming is the secret of the relationship between matter and spirit. We can begin to live our dreams by learning to substitute a positive dream for our previous negative dreams.

Most of us were taught not to fanaticize, but it is important to impress our sub-conscious mind with a fantasy of our desires. Fantasy and reality are not very different, especially when we actually learn that we are creating our lives with our thoughts. Reality is realized fantasy. It is important to not put a cap or limitation on our imagination. Once we have removed our limited thinking and broken the limitation on our imagination, we can create a new reality.

When things do not happen, it is because our thoughts of manifestation lack force. We must create forceful thoughts that stay longer in our consciousness. When we think forceful thoughts over and over, those thoughts will become our desired reality that will come sooner. Remember not to use want and need in your affirmations. For our manifestations to occur, we must stop our limited thinking.

I desire, intend, deserve and now gratefully accept the next unconditional moment to be full of creativity.

I desire, intend, deserve, and am now grateful in the next hour to realize my manifestation of_____.

I desire, intend and now gratefully accept (whatever you desire.)

We can be blocking our blessings through our own limited perceptions of what is possible, what we deserve, or how a thing can happen. We can have everything in the NOW provided that we make a commitment to a different kind of thinking. This is accomplished through the science of spirituality. Spirit is unlimited. It is only matter that is limited. With Spirit everything is possible. We have to bring Spirit consciously and constantly into our lives. Being spiritual means being positive, being unlimited, being joyous forever and ever.

We should ask ourselves several times during the day, "What am I manifesting NOW?"

Most people have been taught to expect to suffer. This is wrong thinking and wrong teaching. When we get connected to our unlimited self, our souls, we experience joy. Something has gone deeply wrong within us if we cannot even wish good things for ourselves. We can change and improve our lives by living spiritual principles. The principles are available to everyone. Spiritual Law and our sub-conscious do not discriminate; it creates what we feed it. Consciousness is everything. We have to take responsibility for what we create and not blame the quality of our lives on anyone else. We are the creators of our own dramas. You are never a victim unless you believe yourself to be a victim. Rather than to complain to others about being a victim, it is important to realize how powerful we are to change our reality. We are the solution, the opportunity, possibilities are unlimited.

If we do not give our desires to God and do only the parts that our soul suggests as our responsibility toward our manifestation, we are playing God, attempting to do everything with our own limited power. We can live our lives as if we do not live in a benevolent universe or we can understand the Law and ask for help from unseen sources and forces. The moment we make the absolute decision "I desire it now," we will begin creating what we ask for. We don't desire to manifest NOW because we are afraid of many things and problems change might cause:

1. We are afraid of success because of its newness and unfamiliarity.
2. Satisfied with the current state of affairs and afraid to venture into something new.
3. Afraid of hurting others.
4. Skeptical of success.
5. Lazy and lack motivation
6. Lack of resources.
7. Lack of qualifications.
8. Afraid of what others will think.
9. Afraid others will be jealous of us.

Everyone should have a plan, but we should also make provision for things to happen momentarily because time is an illusion. We should plan to have it NOW. When we put a wait factor in our beliefs and consciousness, we can stop timeless blessings. The mind wants to proceed in logical sequences. It does not want the end result at the beginning unless we teach it to accept instant manifestation. It is time to make a commitment to a different kind of thinking. In God's consciousness, the thought and its object exist in union. God lives within us as the non-ego consciousness, without any identity whatsoever. We can live in God-consciousness if we get rid of our ego-self. We need to be utterly simple and honest.

True spiritual surrender is a powerful state. What you surrender is your limited ego to the Higher Self or God. This allows for higher intelligence to guide our lives. When we give away our ego, we are giving away something that really doesn't belong to you. It is not who we really are; it is an identity we have made up.

Unfortunately, we love the drama of life and, if we aren't creating enough to make us feel alive in our own lives, we will insert ourselves into the drama of others, read about it, watch it in movies, TV or on the Internet.

We can say we believe in God, but chances are that we believe more in our ego in the World than we do in God. We believe more in what we can see than in what we can't see, but can only feel.

If we are around people who give out affluent, healthy, positive vibrations, then our mind will keep company with those thoughts. If we are with people who produce skeptical, negative thoughts, then we are more likely to begin to think as they do. It is very important to be around people who are positive and harmonious. We need to do what we can to stay as much as possible in harmonious surroundings. This may involve not spending much time with our families, or giving up associations with long time friends if they are constantly in negative drama.

12.

Living in A World Without Limits

You create your life by what you think, feel, believe, fantasize, and act upon. What do you desire? What is the outcome you desire?

Life is an energy game, an opportunity to become crystal clear within you about who and what you choose to be.

The more attached anyone is to other people's opinions, the less authenticity, the less joy and the less spontaneity they will feel. We curse or bless ourselves every moment with our attitudes.

Find the lessons and gifts in every experience.

It takes "chutzpah" to stop making excuses, to need no proof and to need no other justification other than "I AM." The truth of who we are is that God operates *through* our bodies and our personalities. All people are valuable and divine and are meant to live in harmony, balance and love with each other and with nature. It takes time and work before new habits and a whole new way of being is integrated into our energy systems. New beliefs are fragile, but old, fear-ridden beliefs have become habitual through reinforcement.

Feelings create situations; they produce a magnetic energy field that attracts to us circumstances that produce more of the same feelings.

Know that you are one with the ALL. You are the ALL and the everything. Within every cell of your body is the blueprint of life. We are separate by definition and distinct by choice. This separateness and distinction occurs within the Oneness. We are parts, and the parts are each a whole in themselves. Every cell in our body is unique yet still a part of the body, as we are unique, but part of the Oneness.

Thoughts believed become truths, laws and rules through a built-in system called self-fulfilling prophecy. A thought agreed upon by two or more people is called collective reality.

We are programmed from before birth.

We take in beliefs, values, opinions, ideas and ideals from the moment of conception, and perhaps earlier. The moment we enter our bodies we are affected by the consciousness of those around us. We are programmed just as a computer is programmed; by our parents, other family members, our friends and our teachers, by religion, the government and television and other media. The moment you are born you are a customer, a citizen, a potential voter, taxpayer, client, enemy, friend and member of the opposite sex. We are programmed on multiple levels of consciousness, mind, emotions and body. We are open, vulnerable, impressionable beings of pure love, ready to jump into the game of life and play.

Who you believe yourself to be at this moment is the result of that programming unless you have found and begun to de-program yourself. This programming is both an unconscious, non-deliberate action by some people and a conscious, purposeful action by others. According to statistics a child is 60% imprinted with his or her beliefs by the age of two years. Yet, all that can be changed at will.

Whatever we accept as true, absolute, unchanging, real and valid is simply a thought believed. If we change our minds, it's all different. To not know this is to live as a conditioned robot asleep to one's greater Self, known as Spirit. It's all made up in our minds and projected onto the bigger screen of life so that we may experience our own movie.

Our role models are a major part of our programming. A baby (actually a soul) comes to Earth and opens itself to the game called being a Human. If born into a loving, nurturing family environment, a child can become a multifaceted being. If born into a family full or overflowing with fears, neuroses, psychoses, doubts and insecurities, a child has a tremendous amount to overcome. Ignorance of the process of creation through imprinting consciousness and of the power to change this imprinting keeps people enslaved.

We are like sponges absorbing data, Light, color, sound, feelings, thoughts and beliefs. In the first few months of Human life, we learn language, motor control, humor, games and emotion, just to name a few. We learn these things mostly from others, but I believe we come into this life with certain attributes depending on how advanced we were as a soul before we incarnated. We have our soul and our past experiences, which unite with our current and ancestral genetic makeup. We have our parents', siblings', and family's consciousness package to affect us. Genetically speaking, we are the sum total of all life before us. Heredity can be a help or a hindrance depending on the awareness of the self in the body.

I feel we are powerful enough to transcend any limits and to reprogram our entire energy system through intention, love and will power.

The first thing to do is to take responsibility.

We are artists, with life as our canvas. The first step is to listen to what we are thinking and to acknowledge what we currently believe; and then to be willing to change what we think and what we've been taught to believe that may not be true. We need to take responsibility for our pasts and to release what is no longer relevant, anything we no longer desire, and to deliberately program what we now desire.

Think about how you want to feel about yourself, how you want to be, what you want to do. Question every thought, belief, value, ideal, custom, law, rule, concept, principle, and truth by which you live your life. Look at each one as it presents itself in your day-to-day life, and notice how each has affected aspects of your life. Create the thoughts and values that you most desire to have as part of you and deliberately imprint them on all levels of yourself. Next, bring your deepest desires and dreams into your World through your behavior and actions.

I prefer to use the word "desire" rather than want or need. I feel it is more empowering than the word "want" which refers to lack. "Desire" is a word that describes a feeling of passion, excitement, intention and certainty. Our sub-conscious minds and our souls take us literally. When we say we want or need something our sub-conscious and our souls believe we desire to stay in a state of needing and wanting.

What do you desire? What is the outcome you desire?

When the female embraces her male self, she can focus her energy, take action and carry through her visions and desires. When the male accepts his feminine self, he reconnects himself through intuition to the heart of the Universe, allows himself to feel, to love and to express his most magical and creative self.

All people are valuable and divine and are meant to live in harmony, balance and love with each other and nature.

Thoughts believed become truths, laws and rules through a built-in system called self-fulfilling prophecy. A thought agreed upon by two or more people is called a collective reality.

We create our lives by what we think, feel, believe is possible, fantasize and act upon.

Challenge every thought and find your own answers within.

Unless we are aware we have been programmed, we can victimize ourselves. Once we are aware, we can keep what benefits us, release what doesn't serve us, and our purpose, and imprint our highest, most loving thoughts, feelings, beliefs and visions into our lives.

We can, as individuals and as a collective, weed out the programming that causes sickness, crime, low self-esteem, war, premature death and mental illness; and through love we can program the qualities of joy, health, happiness, peace and wealth.

We are not conditioned-response machines. We can be much, much more when we know what makes us tick and what our programming contains.

Repeat to yourself:

I _____ now release any past negative judgments on myself as not being enough.
I love myself and appreciate who I AM.
I now open myself to the thoughts, feelings and beliefs I require to have a beautiful life.

Creating consciousness-reality takes work.

Knowing your thoughts are creative and that you create your own reality is one thing; doing something about it is something else.

You and I are way-showers, visionaries and role models for a new way of being, seeing, sensing, touching, knowing and living.

I AM the creator and cause of whatever I AM experiencing. I can change my life by changing my thoughts and actions.

Once we become aware of our beliefs and thoughts and make the mental, emotional and physical connections, we can alter our experience.

It is easier not to practice our new attitudes and beliefs because it is uncomfortable and confronting. But, if we continue our old habits of living, we will feel unfulfilled.

We can be our own worst enemy or our own best savior.

We can't achieve anything unless we focus on and direct ourselves toward a specific objective. Why do we resist focusing on what we say we really desire? Usually, we have a fear of success, and/or a fear of failure.

Our thoughts, creations, feelings and beliefs must be aligned if we are to experience our full potential. What prevents us from being conscious co-creators is ignorance of who we really are and of the infinite power available to us.

We can change our thoughts, which have a direct impact on our attitude, but until we act upon those thoughts they remain just that, thoughts or good ideas. It isn't easy to change our minds. The ruts are usually very deep. We not only have to change our minds, but we have to develop the skill required in living our newly established beliefs and integrating them into every aspect of our lives.

To transcend our history and release ourselves from ancient programming of fear, self-denial, and the idea of scarcity, we must peel away what we no longer need (fear, self-denial, and the idea of scarcity). What we have left when we give these up is our true, brilliant, beautiful Self.

Whatever we identify with, we become.

The only rights we have are those we give ourselves.

When peace becomes more profitable than war, big business will create peace.

When we are faced with a decision or a choice, it is useful to ask, "Does this empower me and give me greater life, love, joy and freedom to be, do, and have, or does it deny me in any way?"

Chipping away what we do not desire begins with thoughts of what we do desire. What is your true heart's desire?

Transcending our personal history means to own and love our past and to learn from it, but not to be imprisoned, controlled, or limited by it.

Fear of rejection, fear of abandonment, fear of criticism and fear of success or failure can keep us from the joy of freedom that comes from self-expression.

Overcoming our past history occurs the moment we desire to think, believe, feel, or do something not in our past and to create a new and present future. The second part is to actually do the thing itself, one step at a time.

To transcend our past requires desire, action, and risk to imprint a new belief on all levels of our consciousness. Our history can make us bitter or make us stronger. The choice is ours.

Positive change takes as long as it takes, but without action, it will never happen. **The pain, upset or fear we may face is a reflection of the degree to which we are dependent and attached.**

Then was then and now is now.

Find the value in the past experiences, get the lesson of them and move on. Take what they've taught you and move on wiser for it.

Roles are important in the game of life, but it is very important to remember you are greater than any role. You are God playing a role through a Human form.

"Shoulds, ought-tos, have-tos and musts" don't bring forth the best from within us; they repress and limit. Pay attention to what you believe you should do or be, what you must have, do or be, or what you have to do to be accepted.

Try saying to yourself: "I AM capable of being all I can be and at the same time have a loving, intimate, romantic relationship with another person who is whole, kind loving and self-supported and spiritually awake and aware." Do you believe it? Does your body believe it?

Don't spend time analyzing others, just be conscious, exact and clear about your own intentions and desires.

The optimum level of existence is to love yourself and to be centered in a peaceful, neutral position to be able to choose your thoughts, feelings, actions and reactions.

Money is a major Human challenge. It can stand for so many different things:

Energy	Power	Motivation
Love	Value	Reward
Control	Survival	Security
Dreams	Service	Attention
Value		

Peace will come to the World and into our lives when peace, health, joy and beauty become more profitable and important to us than crime, pain, horror and perversion.

We set up struggles to make life feel real and meaningful. We create problems so we can feel smart, rescued, valued or strong.

***It is important to remember we create these challenges
so we can grow.***

Each challenge is a lesson and an opportunity to own or discover more of ourselves. Challenges are self-generated. The key to overcoming any challenge is to know that you can un-create what you no longer desire.

Those who fight the system assure that system will continue. To be against anything gives more energy for it to continue to exist. To remove something undesirable in your life, give your energy, love and attention to what you *do* desire, *not* to what you don't desire. Your enemy exists because you *believe* it is greater than you and you *believe* that it can control or limit you in some way.

What we give out always comes back to us.

If you knew you could not fail, what would you do?

We are brainwashed with conflicting messages.

Who we truly are can't be defined, it can only be experienced.

Dissatisfaction or failure can be the beginning of growth. Life is a game to be played not a sentence to be endured. No person or thing can make you feel anything you don't agree to feel. We determine for ourselves how we choose to feel.

The vast majorities of people in the World cope and survive by following other people's examples. *Stay conscious of who or what you are emulating.*

The Human Earth life is a limitless opportunity to realize who we really are and what we are capable of co-creating with the Source of all life. We have the ability to seek our highest aspirations, desires and revelations and bring them into our lives at whatever level is appropriate.

The Earth has awareness, the Sun and Moon are aware, the planets are aware, everything has a level of awareness and is made of consciousness and energy. All animals, plants, insects, reptiles, birds, rocks, minerals have their own awareness. All of it is creative. Action and evolution are happening constantly. We have the free will to act in harmony with nature and the energy of the Universe. Constant spiritual connection with our soul can lead us into this state of harmony.

Live in a mental and emotional state of gratitude and appreciation for yourself, those you love, what you've learned, where you are and what you have now.

We need to appreciate, acknowledge and care for what we have. Cursing anything about our lives creates setbacks and scarcity. Our energy is directed through thought into the emotional and physical worlds. Physical manifestations are created from our thoughts, concepts, ideas and desire. We live in an ocean of consciousness that is constantly affected by our thoughts and emotions. Stop criticizing and judging, stop arguing, stop making sarcastic comments, and stop wanting and expecting other people to change if you want to be happy. All of this negativity validates the "not enough," "not right" belief, and what we will get is not right and not enough. Cleanse yourself of this negative energy that this self-talk generates.

Keep your agreements. Do not make agreements you don't intend to or can't keep. Stop and think before you agree to anything or sign anything.

Ask your soul for help. We have an infinite wellspring of overflowing supply of guidance, wisdom, and truth available to us from our higher levels of consciousness. Anyone who chooses can contact their own soul. Everyone is qualified for soul communication. The ability is built into our structure.

The more we talk about a problem the larger it will become.

Be enthusiastic about yourself, your life and your purpose. An attitude of expectancy, joy, love and enthusiasm creates an aura of magic and inspires others to work and play with you in the fulfillment of your objectives.

Give love and energy to what is working in your life and focus on your desires, not on problems or what you don't have as of yet. Attitude is everything. It determines the quality of our existence. When we open our mouths and let words come out without thinking or realizing what we are doing, we reinforce erroneous beliefs and perpetrate limitations. Our attitudes offer us a full range of experiences. A closed, fearful attitude offers pain and limitation.

Unfortunately, pessimism is popular, chic and deadly.

Nothing is static. Everything is changing, moving, flowing each and every moment. When we view our lives as living art, one moment flows into the next and each moment can be an exciting adventure. Our attitudes can create blockage or flow. *When creativity stops, disintegration begins.* Attitudes about life, death, time, space and what is real affect the quality of our lives. Our attitudes set the stage for gifts we will experience. Our preconceived expectations and labels limit us and keep us from positive possibilities.

If we do not move graciously, life has a way of pushing or assisting us out of our nest, our comfort zone.

Our attitudes create more of the same attitudes. Attitudes are infectious. Our attitudes affect others. A pessimistic attitude defeats us before we've begun.

Notice you slogans, your witty sayings and fast comebacks—they will give you clues as to how you really feel about your life. Become a practical optimist: one who knows they can be, do and have whatever they desire, but also know it may take time, lasting commitment and a great deal of work to achieve it.

What we resist persists.

Send your light before you to make your path clear. Leave your love and light behind you, leaving spaces better than they were before you came. *Your attitude is a sacred state of mind, body and emotions. It is personal and it is your force field.* As you go about your activities, stay centered within your own field and remember to love yourself. Let other people's garbage bounce off your force field and be recycled as love.

13.

Ideas About Money

Wealth is an attitude of profound trust in oneself and in God. Earth is a classroom for souls to discover and actualize our innate ability to create. We are co-creators with the Creator of the Universe, each other, and nature, and it is time for us to awaken to who we are as creators and to what is possible for all of us when we work in harmony. When we believe we are powerless, we feel hopeless, depressed and angry so we complain, nag, cry and manipulate others.

Wrong ideas about money:

Being wealthy is impossible for us.
There is a limited supply of money.
It is wrong to have what we desire.

Right ideas about money and love:

Know that the supply of good is limitless and infinite.
Know that you are love and you are worth loving. Love attracts. Everything is energy before it becomes a physical object.
Loving yourself and loving life, being excited about your dreams and ideas attracts resources and opportunities.
Whatever the question—love is the answer.
Focus your energy through desire and action.
Wealth is what comes to us in return for our contributions to others.
Knowing what you desire, where you want to go, what you desire to do, what you desire to have focuses your energy into the limitless supply

of the Universe.

Do what you love with excellence and money will follow.

We all have the potential to be geniuses.

Put yourself fully into your creative experience.

Observe how doing what you enjoy can fulfill a need others may have. With modern technology you can sometimes inexpensively live your dreams and serve others through your work and talents.

Ask children "what do you desire to do?" not "what do you want to be?"

We have become addicted to security, attention, approval, status, money, clothes, makeup and bodies instead of remembering who we really are as aspects of God and deciding with our soul how to fulfill our heart's desires, which are the desires of our souls.

Do something for the pure desire of doing it.

When we pinpoint our desires and objectives, our focus and energy is incredibly powerful.

Do whatever you do with excellence. Whatever you do, do it because you want to. Forget about success and failure. Quality and excellence build good feelings inside you and attract positive experiences.

Money follows you if you leave a trail of personal integrity.

When we are committed to what we do, we are absorbed by our passion.

Without commitment there is a tremendous waste or leakage of energy because we are in opposition to ourselves.

Don't concern yourself with, "How will it happen?" Focus only on "What is the next single thing for me to do or know for me to be in a state of Divine Grace?" And then "Just Do It."

Nothing truly wonderful can happen for you unless you are fully open to it, ready for it and willing for it to happen. Keep stepping into love and light and leave fear behind.

You must decide, commit and then just do.

Earth is a place of demonstration where we can practice our beliefs, thoughts and concepts in a physical and experimental framework. Earth is a training ground for creators.

Whatever we are committed to is what will generate and produce.

The moment we become fully committed, the Universe will move in our direction to assist us and miracles and magic become our partners.

Release the hurt of shattered dreams.

Respect yourself whether you have money or not.

True feelings of happiness or self-respect have no direct relationship to material things.

We have shattered dreams that we believe were caused by our not having enough money or by our family or loved ones not providing for us as we wanted to be provided for.

Survival is not the purpose for living; thriving and flourishing is.

Have you blended self-worth and money?

Are you worthy? Good enough?

Is it wrong for you to be wealthy? Who will be upset?

Do you believe you will lose the love of others or that they will not love you for yourself?

Do you believe there isn't enough for everyone?

Do you believe you don't have enough time or energy or that men or parents should take care of you?

Do you fear ending up alone?

If you believe any or all of these things, you are setting up your life to prove you are right.

We simply have to like the feeling of wealth, love and power more than feeling poor, wretched, unloved and weak. We have previously traded our power for love and pseudo security.

Learn to use money for the intention it was created—a system of exchange of service for service.

We create our dreams by feeling and doing; having looks like the objective, but feeling and doing are the fun and true objective.

Support yourself *on all levels.*

Think and see yourself as you desire to be. See, smell, taste, feel your co-creations and they will appear. See and describe in writing the end result you desire in great detail and then release it to the Universe with: "I now accept this or something better, through the grace of God and to the highest good of all concerned."

Ask yourself: "What do I need to do or know to have my desire happen in harmony with the divine will of love?"

If our bodies have pain, it is a result of emotional pain we have stored.

We can reprogram ourselves into being loving, caring, healthy, happy, wealthy, and responsible divine beings, co-creating paradise, beauty and heaven on Earth.

Learn to live the win/win principle. Win/win is the opposite of the belief that if someone wins someone else loses.

Life is about contribution. Whatever you want to share—give it to yourself first.

Universal energy is designed to flow through us. If we believe in scarcity of love or money we hold on too tight to what we have and impede this flow.

Money is just energy and needs to flow to serve us, others and our creations.

Money exists—mentally, move it where you desire it to be.

Prosperity is an attitude of plenty. Prosperity is a feeling of oneness with the ongoing flow of life energy. Open yourself up to giving what you desire to receive; if it is respect or appreciation give it to yourself first before you can receive it from outside you.

By taking care of children in adulthood, we delay their maturity and promote weakness.

Money is not the purpose. It is the supportive energy. Who you are as a person is your gift.

Money is pay for the value of what you do, not for what you as a person are worth. You are worth much more than money.

Giving and receiving represent inflow and outflow of energy.

Money keeps us accountable.

Spend less than you earn.

Money is energy exchange.

Keep records.

Pay bills and taxes.

Save some as a cushion.

Invest in yourself.

Contribute or tithe to something you believe in or what inspires you.

Set spending limits for yourself.

Know where you are financially at all times.

Be clear about what money is and what it isn't.

Put your attention on the value you are offering energetically.

Correct when you are in error—be persistent—we tend to give up too quickly.

Persistence is our continual movement toward our objective. Correction is what we need to do when we find our action or inaction did not achieve our desired goal. Get back on track as soon as possible without any self-condemnation.

It is no big deal to make a mistake. Mistakes are essential to discovery and learning of any kind. We must be free to experiment, explore, discover and invent. In fact, if we are not making any mistakes we are staying too comfortable and not taking risks. We are programmed to fear both failure and success. We find ourselves stuck in neutral and frustrated. There is a great deal of pressure from the masses for us to conform. *Refuse to be a conformist.*

Most of us want approval so much that the slightest disapproval can send us into guilt, embarrassment, hiding and self-judgment. Self-defeat is the only defeat.

Take care of what you have and live in a constant state of gratitude. What we don't appreciate disappears. What you love and care for blesses you.

Living in a constant state of gratitude and appreciation transforms our daily existence into an adventure full of treasures and surprises.

Adjust from being a consumer to being a caretaker.

Be grateful for being alive. Start each day with a feeling of appreciation for the day, the people in your life, yourself and the gifts you are about to receive.

Communicate clearly. Promote who you are and what you have to offer. Listen to what others need and desire. Can you help? Provide service with a commitment to excellence.

ANGER IS CONFUSING

Learn to express your anger without hurting anyone.

We've been taught that if we feel anger, we are wrong.

If we express it, we are bad.

If we stuff it, we will become depressed.

All anger is justified by the person feeling it. We can be justified or we can be happy, but we can't be both.

Anger is a feeling that comes when we believe we have been hurt, disappointed, used, threatened, ignored, attacked or rejected.

Everything we did, or the power we gave away, we did by choice at the time even if it feels like we didn't have a choice. We always have a choice.

If we let the people around us repress us, then we become angry. The anger is either exploding and creating destruction, or seething below the surface and oozing out into illness, depression or self-pity.

TRUTH IS A FUNCTION OF HEALTH.

Take a look at your anger, frustration and resentment or depression and see where you have created being stopped, repressed, abused, denied, punished or kept from being, doing or having what you desire in any way. Our obstacles are self-generated.

Anger is an automatic reaction when one feels attacked, ignored, discounted, stopped, thwarted or contradicted.

Anger is energy that has stopped flowing and is piled up waiting to blow up.

Victims love to feel hurt, rejected, used, unappreciated, unacknowledged.

What better way to attempt to control the people around you than to pretend you are not creating whatever is happening in your life.

Live as you desire and generate what is important to you.

Discover the games you've been playing and admit your payoff or benefit. Is it worth the cost to your self-esteem?

> **People, especially children, learn by example**
> **not by what you tell them.**

Two of the books that have inspired me and helped me the most in my spiritual and emotional growth are by Terry Cole-Whittaker. I highly recommend them to you: *WHAT YOU THINK OF ME IS NONE OF MY BUSINESS AND LOVE AND POWER IN A WORLD WITHOUT LIMITS.*

> **Bless you on your journey of self-discovery.**